THE WINNING GRACE

SAM UHUNOMA

THE WINNING GRACE

HOW I WON AND AM STILL WINNING

CHALFANT ECKERT
PUBLISHING

The Winning Grace

Copyright © 2016 Sam Uhunoma. All Rights Reserved.

No rights claimed for public domain material, all rights reserved. No parts of this publication may be reproduced, stored in any retrieval system, or transmitted in any form or by any means, electronic, mechanical, recording, or otherwise, without the prior written permission of the author. Violations may be subject to civil or criminal penalties.

Library of Congress Number: 2016932573

ISBN: 978-1-63308-214-4 (paperback)
       978-1-63308-215-1 (ebook)

Cover and Interior Design by R'tor John D. Maghuyop

1028 S Bishop Avenue, Dept. 178
Rolla, MO 65401

Printed in the United States of America

TABLE OF CONTENTS

Acknowledgements 7

About The Book 9

Introduction 11

Chapter One: Saved By Grace 15

Chapter Two: Justified By Grace 23

Chapter Three: Made Righteous By Grace 33

Chapter Four: The Empowerment Of Grace 45

Chapter Five: Grace Channels 57

Chapter Six: Grace For Service 77

Chapter Seven: The Spirit Of Grace 85

Chapter Eight: Grace Guarantees Abundant Life 95

Conclusion 105

About The Author 107

ACKNOWLEDGEMENTS

First and foremost, I would like to express my profound gratitude to God Almighty for Divine wisdom, revelation, knowledge, understanding and inspiration to write this book. Also, I want to say a big thanks to my family: my parents, siblings and relatives for their support and words of encouragement towards actualising my dreams. I have grown spiritually over time because of the places God positioned me for spiritual growth. So, I will not fail to mention these wonderful churches. House of the King (Royal House International Ministries) in Nigeria, Mountain of Fire (Nigeria), Heaven's Intervention Fire Ministries (Nigeria), Winners Chapel (Nigeria) and Winners Chapel International, Manchester. I want also to thank the wonderful friends I met in Winners Chapel International, Manchester, who encouraged me. Thanks to all my mentors, May God bless you all.

ABOUT THE BOOK

Until I realised what grace was and how to apply it to my personal life, I struggled with sin. I had a battle with sin but desired a way out of it. I tried coming out of it on my own, but it was not working. I knew there must be a way out somehow, but I didn't know how it works. I decided to seek a solution. I found my answers in God's grace. I came to an understanding of what grace is and started maximizing it in my life. I won the battle against sin. I am still winning today because I have gotten what it takes to win and that's the principles this book aim to reveal to you how to stand strong in the face of opposition. To be steadfast, immovable and unshakable in faith. Continuing in sin after receiving grace is an abuse of grace. Shall we continue in sin, that grace may abound? God forbid. This book is flooded with revelations that will transform your life and teach you how to practically engage God's grace for result oriented life.

This book reveals how you can live a balanced Christian life. From the point of your salvation to the point of your glorification, God wants you to live a life full of glory. He has planned abundant life in His grace for you. I have enjoyed supernatural favour by mixing faith with God's grace for abundance.

My perspective on life and my thinking patterns were transfigured by the revelation of God's Word. I explained some of these revelations and how they apply to my journey of life thus far. I shared these revelations using biblical scriptures, quotes, dialogues and personal testimonies to give you a better understanding. God is the inspiration behind the contents of this book. I only attempt to put down what He has inspired me to write. I am not writing as one that has arrived but as Paul would say, I press toward the mark for the prize of the high calling of God in Christ Jesus. I am pressing with the same principles I have revealed in this book. I still practice what I preach daily because on earth growing in grace is inevitable. You cannot outgrow the grace of God upon your life. I trust God to bless you richly as you read along.

INTRODUCTION

What is grace? **GRACE** stands for **G**od's **R**eliable **A**bundance by **C**hrist's **E**ffort. Grace is from God and not from works. Grace is reliable because its source is reliable. God's grace is abundant. It's totally a product of Christ's effort, not your efforts. Grace is not merely unmerited favour; it's far more than that. Unmerited favour is an accompanist of God's grace. It's an integral part of grace but not all there is to grace.

Grace is a huge package from God that has diverse by-products. Grace is delivered to us by Jesus Christ through faith. Grace does not cover sin. Grace reveals sin and gives you the ability to withstand it. Grace is not a license to sin, but empowerment to overcome sin. Grace gives you leverage above sin and does not license you to keep sinning.

> *That he would grant you according to the riches of his glory, to be strengthened with might by his Spirit in the inner man.*
> EPHESIANS 3:16

Grace is God's enabling strength in your inner man to do things beyond your human strength. It's a supernatural empowerment bestowed on your spirit through the Holy Spirit.

Strength and power go with God's grace and makes you act supernaturally in the natural. In other words, there is such power beyond human strength to perpetually overcome sin. It's not grace if sin still abounds. Grace gives a total checkout to sin. Grace is a resistor to sin and the capability to see the kingdom of God made manifest in your life on earth.

> *And he said unto me, My grace is sufficient for thee; for my strength is made perfect in weakness.*

INTRODUCTION

***Most gladly therefore will I rather glory in my infirmities,
that the power of Christ may rest upon me.***
2 Corinthians 12:9

God's grace speaks of his strength made perfect in your weakness. Paul said, "I celebrate; I make known my weakness so that the power of Christ (Grace) may rest upon me."

Know that grace is only relevant on earth, after death no more grace. In heaven, there is no grace. Heaven is the destination of *grace-full* people. In heaven, you don't need grace to live supernaturally above sin and the devil because there is no sin. There is no devil to fight over there. You just naturally live holy and enjoy abundance without any contest!

You are saved by grace through faith. What saves you, sustains your salvation till you meet with your Saviour in His second coming. Abundant grace has been made available for you to be saved on earth. Use it wisely while it last.

Grace is the operation of God in the heart of man effected via the agency of the Spirit of Grace (The Holy Spirit).

In this glorious kingdom of God, where we belong. We must begin to reckon ourselves as little children who look unto their father in loving confidence for every benefit. It can be for the pardon so freely given or for the enabling strength that comes from Him who works in us both to will and to do of His good pleasure (***Philippians 2:13 says For it is God which worketh in you both to will and to do of his good pleasure***).

Know also that all things are yours for the taking under grace. In God's grace, you are entitled to all the abundant supply that God has made available in Christ Jesus. God's grace guarantees all resounding success in life. Grace is your advantage to live an abundant life on earth (***John 10:10)***. Take full advantage of it.

It's heart-warming to know, appreciate and maximize the grace of God in our walk with Christ.

This book is an eye-opener to the winning grace that will make your service to Almighty God flow with freshness and uncommon zeal. It will invigorate your spirit for greater performance.

I see you emerge a winner as you go through the winning grace in Jesus name Amen.

QUOTES

God's grace is amazing! We're saved by grace - God's undeserved favour - and we live by grace, which is also God's power in our lives to do what we could never do in our own strength.
And it's all because God is love, and He loves us unconditionally, constantly and completely.
Joyce Meyer

Amazing grace! How sweet the sound,
that saved a wretch like me! I once was lost but now am found, was blind but now I see… Through many dangers,
toils and snares, I have already come; 'Tis grace has brought me safe thus far, and grace will lead me home.
John Newton

Faith is a living, daring confidence in God's grace, so sure and certain that a man could stake his life on it a thousand times.
Martin Luther

CHAPTER ONE

SAVED BY GRACE

*For by grace are ye saved through faith,
that not of yourselves; It is the gift of God.*
EPHESIANS 2:8

G race saves us through faith. In other words; grace is made available by God, but obtainable through faith. An awareness of the availability of a thing does not mean you can have it in your hand. It means you know it exists, and it is available. Knowing the availability of a thing does not automatically deliver it to your hand. Your only access to grace is faith. Faith in God's grace is what brings salvation, not your works or efforts. You did not deserve it, but God bestowed it on you. You didn't earn it; Christ earned it for you. No amount of works would have made you worthy of receiving this grace. It is the gift of God.

*For the grace of God,
that bringeth salvation hath appeared to all men.*
TITUS 2:11

Your salvation is a product of grace. The appearance of grace is to bring salvation to all men. Without grace, there is no salvation. God's grace has been made open to all men, but only those that dive in through faith can access and obtain it.

> *In whom we have redemption through his blood,*
> *the forgiveness of sins, according to the riches of his grace.*
> Ephesians 1:7

God is a God of sacrifice; God sacrificed his son to make us sacred. Redemption was the price God paid to manifest his grace and adopted us as sons. You and I were bought with a price through the blood of Jesus Christ. Redemption breeds salvation. You would not have experienced salvation without the price for it. God paid the price (Redemption), and we received the prize (Salvation).

> *For God so loved the world, that he gave his only begotten*
> *son, that whosoever believeth in him should not perish,*
> *but have everlasting life.*
>
> *For God sent not his son into the world to condemn the world;*
> *but that the world through him might be saved.*
> John 3:16-17

God's love for us propelled him to pay the price by giving his son (His only begotten son). Jesus in obedience to the father went to the cross and died, after contending with the devil. He won the prize for us to be saved. He is our Saviour. His name means Saviour. All you need to receive this prize is to believe. God gave the price; Jesus won the prize for us to be saved.

Redemption through his blood means to be delivered from the power and influence of the devil through the blood of Jesus. Salvation became obtainable when the blood was shared on the cross. Forgiveness of sins follows.

You will agree with me that the value you pay for a thing determines how protective you are about that thing. Think for a moment! If man can place value on the things they buy according to the price they paid for it, why can't God? You mean so much to Him dear valued ones!

The price God paid to get you saved is inestimable. God loves you dear valued ones. It does not matter what you have done, where you have been, what matters is His fixed and unchanging love for you. His love is fixed; He will not love you less than He has ever loved you. Even when you think your sin is unpardonable, his love is still the same. He is ever loving. The massiveness of your sin does not change his love for you.

Christ death for your sin was a once forever done deal. He died once for your past, present and future sins.

> *By the which will we are sanctified through the offering of the body of Jesus Christ once for all.*
>
> *But this man, after he had offered one sacrifice for sins for ever, sat down on the right hand of God.*
>
> *For by one offering he hath perfected for ever them that are sanctified.*
> HEBREWS 10:10, 12 & 14

Remember, you were yet a sinner when God made the sacrifice for your salvation.

> *But God commendeth his love towards us, in that while we were yet sinners, Christ died for us.*
> ROMANS 5:8

God does not visit your past to bless you. God does not see past records as men do. He only sees you in the present which is in Christ. While you were yet a chronic sinner, he displayed his love towards you.

What on earth do you think can change his love for you? Nothing! God treasures you.

God's love does not fluctuate. It is steadfast love. Stop looking at how huge your sins are, but how huge His love is towards you. Turn to your lover (God) today and he will rescue you and give you the grace to stand.

God loves sinners! God certainly does not love sin, but He loves the individual. There is no depth of sin committed by a sinner that can prevent the arm of God from saving the sinner who seeks forgiveness.

If God would save a murderer like Saul (who later became Apostle Paul), then He will save anybody. If God would save an adulterer like David, then he will save anybody. If God would save a drunkard like Noah, then he will save anybody.

No saint was not once a sinner, and no sinner does not have the potential of becoming a saint. God can use any sinner, who will yield to His call and forget his past failures. If you are not born again, this is an avenue you must not joke with.

> ***Wherefore I give you to understand, that no man speaking by the Spirit of God calleth Jesus accursed: and that no man can say that Jesus is the Lord, but by the Holy Ghost.***
> 1 Corinthians 12:3

The Holy Spirit is at work now. He is the Spirit of Grace. The Spirit of Grace is the reaping Spirit on earth today. Reaping the unsaved into the Kingdom of God. He wants the unsaved to be saved. He is ever-ready to release the saving grace. You need faith to maximize the grace He carries for you. All you need is to be willing. He is ever-willing, the question is, are you willing?

Salvation is available; you just have to be willing to receive it.

ACCESS TO GRACE THROUGH FAITH

Without faith, there is no salvation.

> *For by grace are ye saved through faith;*
> *and that not of yourselves; it is the gift of God: Not of works,*
> *lest any man should boast.*
> EPHESIANS 2:8-9

Faith in God's grace is the requirement for your salvation. Salvation is not a product of yourself. It is not a product of your works. Therefore, you can't take credit for it. It's all God's work!

We are privileged! Let your boast be on God, not on self because you can't be saved nor get anybody saved independently of God. Your faith is the only requirement needed for you to access his grace for salvation.

Salvation is a product of grace made manifest by faith. Saving grace is accessible by saving faith. Grace is a gift from God, a gift that must be accepted by its recipient. Your only acceptance fee for grace is faith. Saving faith is just a faith needed for you to obtain salvation. It is not all there is to faith! You are to live continuously by faith. Faith work starts with you and ends with you while grace work starts with God and ends with God.

> *Not for that we have dominion over your faith,*
> *but are helpers of your joy; for by faith ye stand.*
> 2 CORINTHIANS 1:24

You are saved by faith and stand by faith. Having been saved by grace through faith, your continuous standing is made possible by faith also.

> *Now the just shall live by faith; but if any man draw back,*
> *my soul shall have no pleasure in him.*
> HEBREWS 10:38

To live by faith means to have enough faith, such that it sustains your existence. Your faith is your life sustenance. God has saved you. You are to guard your salvation jealously by your faith.

God has given you a new life by giving you a gift of grace. Now that you are saved, you need to live continuously in this new existence by your faith. Therefore, your faith needs to grow steadily.

You need to grow in faith through God's Word. Make it your lifestyle, because it's your life sustenance. Grace saves us. This grace is obtainable through faith. Saving faith is the requirement needed to maximize the saving grace. You need faith to draw the virtues in grace. You need faith to explore the content of grace. Grace depends on faith to deliver maximally. The grace of God is a gift of love towards you. All you need to do is to receive it. Then you are saved!

If you know you are not born again, this is an opportunity you cannot afford to miss. You can be in church and still miss out on the saving grace of God. It doesn't matter how long you have been in church; what matters is if you are in touch with the saving power of God's grace. Check yourself inwardly. You might have made mistakes and slid away; it's time to retrace your steps and come back to your lover. He loves you and has been waiting for your decision to invite Him. He has shown His love as a loving father; it's time for you to acknowledge Him and accept Him in your life. Your future is a direct product of every wise decision you make. The grace of God that brings salvation is a gift, but receiving this gift is a choice you have to make. Make this decision and transform your life forever. Please say the following prayers:

Heavenly Father,

I come to You admitting that I am a sinner. Right now, I choose to turn away from sin, and I ask You to cleanse me of all unrighteousness. I believe that Your Son, Jesus, died on the cross to take away my sins. I also believe that He rose again from the dead so that I might be forgiven of my sins and made righteous through faith in Him. I call upon the name of Jesus Christ to be the Savior and Lord of my life. Jesus, I choose to follow You and ask that You fill me with the power of the Holy Spirit. I declare that right now I am a child of God. I am free from sin and full of the righteousness of God. I am saved in Jesus' name. Amen.

(Source: www.harrisonhouse.com/client/client_pages/salvation.cfm).

If you have genuinely prayed this prayer. Congratulation, you are saved. Today is a special day in your life. Heaven is rejoicing over you right now. Your destiny is opened up; you are in for a glorious destiny in Christ. Please look for a Bible believing Church and be baptized, and continually grow in the Word of God's grace that can build you up and to give you an inheritance among the sanctified.

PRE-CHAPTER CONVERSATION

Sam: Hello brother John.

John: Hi Sam.

Sam: How are you?

John: I am fine, thank you. And you?

Sam: I am fine, thanks. Hope all is well?

John: Sure all is well. Why are you asking?

Sam: I have observed for some time, that there is a change in your attitude to service and worship to God. Is there anything, you would like to share with me? Is there anything eating you up? Are you worried about something? I am asking so that you can free yourself of any burden hindering your relationship with God.

John: Thanks for your concern. I have done some unspeakable things that I am not happy about. I feel very bad and unworthy to worship God. So much guilt have clouded my mind, which I find it difficult to even lift my hands in worship to God. Whenever I feel like ignoring them even in the Church, the devil keeps bringing a flashback of everything I have done. He keeps telling me, look at you. You are standing to worship as if you are a saint.

Sam: Oh dear! I understand how you feel. I have been there, I have made some mistakes and felt so bad about them. But I did not allow my mistakes to take me away from God nor dictate my worship. Mistake means you miss and take [miss take]. In other words, you took the wrong thing, step or direction instead of the right thing. All you need is a retake, just start taking the right things, right actions and directions. Grace has justified you. The sense of guilt you feel is a trick of the devil to steal the Joy of your salvation. If he can steal your Joy, he will bring you into condemnation and gradually take you away from God.

To buttress my point, let's see in the next chapter what it means to be justified by grace.

CHAPTER TWO

JUSTIFIED BY GRACE

Being justified freely by his grace through the redemption that is in Christ Jesus; whom God hath set forth to be a propitiation through faith in his blood, to declare his righteousness for the remission of sins that are past, through the forbearance of God.

ROMANS 3:24-25

Your justification came as a result of the redemption package. The grace of our Lord Jesus is the reason we can stand before God without any sense of guilt. By the law of sin and death, we were doomed to condemnation. We were helpless, hopeless and frustrated, but by His grace and mercy, He has found us and justified us. We can now stand with head upright looking unto Jesus, the author and finisher of our faith. Jesus gave his righteousness to us, for our sins to be wiped away. Therefore, we should no longer be holding on to our guilt to serve God, but coming to our loving father with a guiltless attitude. Lawbreakers can be punished; sinners are bound to be punished for their sins. There is no consequence for your past sins because somebody has been punished already and that person is Jesus, Your Saviour!

JUSTIFIED BY GRACE

Jesus demonstrated grace. He did not come to judge or to condemn, but to forgive save and justify.

Justified is a legal term use in a secular court of criminal law. To be justified in a court of criminal law means to be acquitted, declared innocent, and declared not guilty. In the Bible, it means even more. It means to be declared righteous, to have a righteous standing before God. In other words; you are appearing before God as one that has never done anything wrong.

To be justified means that in the sight of God you are just and had never committed any sin. Grace brings justification. Justification is that divine judicial pronouncement that you are innocent of any guilt and declared righteous through the work of Christ. Justification is made possible by grace. The justifier (Jesus) has made you justified in him.

In God's grace, there is no condemnation, and there is no sinner. What we have is justification. Grace justifies you; it does not punish you for your sins like the law does. Grace erases all your sins, cleanses you and brings you before God as if you had never done any wrong.

You are appearing before God as a sinless person, because of what His sinless Son Jesus Christ did on the Cross. Jesus was held responsible for the crime you committed.

God is a merciful God, He had mercy on us, that's why He made a provision for Christ to pay for what we did. Jesus Christ paid for what we did and made us free from the consequences that follow our acts. We are free to serve God Almighty now, without consequences of sins and death.

Mercy means not receiving the penalties for your actions as deserved. Mercy said no to the death penalties of your sins. Stop thinking that you are punished for the sins you have committed. God does not have a record booklet for those sins anymore, let alone punishing you for them. If God is punishing you, why did He send His only begotten son to be punished for your sins? Stop pointing finger at God thinking He is behind your predicament due to your sins. It's the trick of the devil to keep you away from God. God can never punish you for your sins. All He needed to do, to eradicate condemnation and declare you justified has been done already through Christ.

God can never visit your past to bless your present and future. All that you will ever need, He had made available. And He will not start marking register to see if you did right enough to be qualified for His blessings. Jesus has made you qualified for His blessings. The redemption plan was a plan B, made by God after Adam failed in plan A. This plan was for all.

> ***For God so loved the world, that he gave his only begotten son, that whosoever believeth in him should not perish but have everlasting life.***
> JOHN 3:16

God's love propelled him to send his only begotten son to die for the sins of the whole world. He did not restrict it to a particular set of people. It was a general plan B, but only believers can enjoy it. Until you become a believer, you can still be under all sort of oppressions of the devil because you are of the world. In Christ, you are in the world, but not of the world. Your life is no longer tied to the evil happenings in the world.

> ***Ye are of God, little children, and have overcome them: because greater is he that is in you, than he that is in the world.***
> 1 JOHN 4:4

As an unbeliever, what God did was for you also. All you need to do is to receive him. Allow him into your heart. He will save you if you are willing and ready. God's love is constant and does not change because of what you have done or what you will do.

Even as an unbeliever, God is not punishing you for anything. The devil is only taking advantage of your unwillingness to surrender to God, to afflict you and bring you under condemnation.

> *He that believeth on him is not condemned;*
> *but he that believeth not is condemned already, because he*
> *hath not believed in the name of the only begotten son of God*
>
> *And this the condemnation, that light is come into the world,*
> *and men loved darkness rather than light,*
> *because their deed were evil.*
> JOHN 3:18-19

You are not yet justified if you are not a believer. It takes believing to become justified. Run and take cover under grace and mercy. Jesus loves you; He is beckoning on you. Come to him and receive Him as your personal Lord and Saviour. In Christ, there is no condemnation. What Christ did is only effective in your life when you are in him. You are justified only in Christ Jesus. Outside Christ, you are doomed to condemnation because you are still in darkness. Coming into Christ brings light and takes away condemnation.

> *Not by works of righteousness which we have done,*
> *but according to his mercy he saved us, by the washing of*
> *regeneration and renewing of the Holy Ghost;*
>
> *Which he shed on us abundantly through*
> *Jesus Christ our Saviour;*
>
> *That being justified by his grace, we should be made heirs*
> *according to the hope of eternal life.*
> TITUS 3:5-7

God's mercy saved you. Think about where you would have been outside of his mercy! Mercy is not receiving the penalties for your actions as deserved while Grace is receiving what you don't deserve. They are twain sisters. Grace excludes merit. Humanity does not deserve salvation, but grace made it possible. You can't earn pardon for sins by works of human righteousness. If such were the case, you could boast of your redemption. However, it's none of your inputs but all of His. All the glory belongs to Him.

You were regenerated and made new again by the Holy Ghost just as if you have never sinned. You are being justified by grace and declared heirs according to the hope of eternal life. Hallelujah! Praise God forevermore!

> *So then, it is not of him that willeth, nor of him that runneth but of God that that showeth mercy.*
> ROMANS 9:16

God's shows his mercy to you not because of your works but because of his will. God shows His mercy to you not because of your will, or because you are fervent, but because he has decided to show mercy in Christ Jesus. Your role is to accept the mercy of God. When you appreciate God's mercy in your life, you will have multiple compassion in return.

> *Let us therefore come boldly unto the throne of grace that we may obtain mercy and find grace to help in time of need.*
> HEBREWS 4:16

Let us draw near boldly without fear nor trembling unto the throne of grace (A throne where all grace abounds) that we might take mercy and find grace to help in time of need. Man born of a woman is always in need. Needs keep arising day after day. The grace to help in time of need is in the throne of grace. You need the confidence to access this throne of grace. This confidence ultimately comes from being justified by grace. Confidence means the absence of guilt which creates boldness. Your confidence before God in the place of prayer gives you access to obtain mercy and to receive more grace to help in time of need. For you to find, you must seek, the instrument by which you seek is faith that is devoid of fear or guilt.

Adam brought condemnation to mankind, but Christ brought justification. You are justified in Christ Jesus. Hallelujah!

> ***By the deeds of the law, there shall no flesh be justified in God's sight; for the law is the knowledge of sin.***
> ROMANS 3:20

The law could only condemn, not justify. In-law could not justify us before God, but out-law in Christ has justified us before God. Hallelujah!

> ***Who shall lay anything to the charge of God's elect? It is God that justifieth.***
>
> ***Who is he that condemneth? It is Christ that died, yea rather, that is risen again, who is even at the right hand of God, who also maketh intercession for us.***
> ROMANS 8:33-34

God has justified you, no one is permitted to lay any charge on you. If you listen to the voices of the people around you, you will feel condemned. People can always remind you of your past life and discourage your present living. You don't have to listen to people for any reason, because whom the Son of God has set free is free indeed! Stop listening to people's report and start listening to God' report about you.

> ***When Jesus had lifted up himself, and saw none but the woman, he said unto her, woman, where are those thine accusers? Hath no man condemned thee?***
>
> ***She said, No man, Lord. And Jesus said unto her, Neither do I condemn thee; go, and sin no more.***
> JOHN 8:10-11

Dear valued ones, it is crucial you realize how free you are in Christ. Not free to engage in sinful acts, but free from the condemnation of your past sins. This freedom is what will make you an overcomer over your weaknesses, destructive habits and addictions. Which in turn makes you relate and fellowship with your lovely father easily. If you feel that God condemns you for your failures, running to him for help would not be an option. Instead, you will want to run away from him. Run back to Jesus, who has taken your condemnation on the cross. *He told that woman, Neither do I condemn thee; go and sin no more.* People might condemn you, but God can never condemn you. People might forsake God, but God can never forsake you. People might make you feel like the worst sinner, but God will make feel loved, cherished and treasured. If only you are repentant.

> ***There is therefore now no condemnation to them which are in Christ Jesus, who walk not after the flesh, but after the Spirit.***
> ROMANS 8:1

There is no condemnation in Christ. If you are in Christ, you are free from condemnation. The worst condemnation that can befall a believer is self-condemnation. Your heart can condemn you; heart condemnation is self-condemnation. If a man is condemned by his heart, it means guilt has taken over him. Your conscience is a faculty of your heart; that is the voice of your heart. Don't bring condemnation upon yourself by yourself, because no condemnation is permitted in your life in Christ Jesus. Thinking of your past deeds and feeling as if you are being punished for them can bring condemnation. Jesus Christ is not holding anything against you.

> ***If your heart does not condemn you, then you can have confidence to live above condemnation. It also goes a long way to determine how you approach God.***
> 1 JOHN 3:20-21

> ***Holding the mystery of faith in a pure conscience.***
> 1 TIMOTHY 3:9

In other words, holding the secret of faith in a clean conscience. The mystery (secret) of faith delivers maximally in a pure conscience. Let your conscience be devoid of every guilt because of your knowledge of what Christ has done for you. If your conscience is guilt-free, then you can lay hold on the mystery of faith. Your conscience is the tool the devil uses to speak to you, putting you in remembrance of what you have done in time past. Grace justifies you!

John: Awesome.

Sam: Hope you have been blessed?

John: Yes, I have been blessed.

Sam: Hope to see you at the next meeting.

Take home prayer point: Father, I thank you for the justification that comes with your grace. Thank you for causing me to free myself of every guilt. Thank you for there is no more condemnation for me in Christ Jesus. I am free indeed and empowered by your grace to live in this reality in Jesus name. Amen.

PRE-CHAPTER CONVERSATION

Sam: Hey. Good to see you! How is your spiritual life going? How is your relationship with God? Hope your service and worship to God is flowing with freshness and excitement now?

John: Oh yeah. My spiritual life is growing from glory to glory! I am having a wonderful time in God's presence whenever I go to church. I have an intimate relationship with God, and I am very excited to know that grace justified me and freed me from guilt.

Sam: That's great news. Can you boldly say, you are righteous?

John: Wait a minute, let me check the list of the things I do righteously to determine that. I still need to examine myself.

Sam: You have been made righteous in Christ by grace, and you have been imparted with righteousness to bear righteous fruits.

John: How can I possibly say I am righteous when I know that sometimes I do unrighteous things? I am not perfect, so I am not righteous. Only Jesus Christ is righteous because He is perfect. He did not sin at all when He was here on earth.

Sam: This righteousness has nothing to do with your works. It's a function of Christ's work for you. So, as He is so are you now! You have won righteousness that you did not work for. You are perfect before God irrespective of what you have done, because of the sacrifice Jesus paid.

John: If that's the case. How do I walk in this reality?

Sam: Nice question. All you need to assume this state of righteousness is faith. You need faith to become as righteous as God and also to be imparted to bear the fruits of righteousness.

Do you have an account with any bank?

John: Yes I do.

Sam: Do you receive an alert?

John: Yes, I subscribed for the alert.

Sam: If I worked and earned money. Then paid the money into your account, for you to enjoy for free. Then you received an alert on your phone. Do you need to work again to enjoy that money?

John: No! I will just go to the bank and withdraw the money.

Sam: In the same manner, righteousness has been paid into your account without your righteous works, and you are empowered to use it as well. Your ATM card or withdrawal's slip is your faith. You withdraw and start spending it by acting righteously.

Let's see how this transaction took place. How you have been made righteous by grace.

CHAPTER THREE

MADE RIGHTEOUS BY GRACE

For He (God) hath made him (Christ),
to be sin for us, who knew no sin; that we might be made the
righteousness of God in him (Jesus Christ).
2 CORINTHIANS 5:21

We were once in sin; Jesus was in righteousness. We were sinners, Jesus was a righteous man who knew no sin. He left His righteousness identity to identify with our sins and made us identify with His righteousness. There was a great exchange made on the cross; Christ was a righteous man, who knew no sin, but was made sin because of you and I. Unrighteousness was placed on Him so that His righteous nature can be unleashed on you. He killed your unrighteousness to the cross and gave his righteousness to you. He died as a sinner on the cross, for you to live as a sinless man on earth. He died as any unrighteous man might have died, for you to live a righteous life.

You were made righteous by grace. God does not see you as a sinner; He sees you through the lens of the cross of His Son (Jesus Christ).

When God looks at you, what he sees, is the price he paid. In Christ Jesus, you are not the unrighteous trying to become righteous. You are righteous; the devil is trying to make you unrighteous. The good news is as far as you are in Christ, what He did for you cannot be undone. You might sin, you might make mistakes, but that does not change the nature Christ has given to you. It only cast stains on your new nature.

What do you do to stains? You clean them up and forge ahead. Come to God as you are, confess your sins and He will clean you up.

> *If we confess our sins, he is faithful and just to forgive us our sins, and to cleanse us from all unrighteousness).*
> 1 JOHN 1:9

> *Wherefore, as by one man sin entered into the world and death by sin; and so death passed upon all men, for that all have sinned.*
> ROMANS 5:12

Sin entered into the world through Adam and death accompanied sin. Death was passed upon all men. Adam's sin had a universal effect; one man's sin had an effect upon all men. In the same vein, one righteous man released all men from eternal death. What Jesus did has a universal effect also. Its effect becomes evident in the lives of those who entered into it by faith. Only those who have subscribed to the Lordship of Jesus Christ are made righteous.

> *For if through the offence of one many be dead, much more the grace of God, and the gift by grace, which is by one man, Jesus Christ, hath abounded unto many.*
> ROMANS 5:15

> *For as by one man's disobedience many were made sinners, so by the obedience of one shall many be made righteous.*
> ROMANS 5:19

Through one man, sin brought death to many. But much more is the grace of God towards us. The gift of righteousness, which is a by-product of grace exceeds the consequences of sin. Jesus obtained the prize (gift of righteousness) by paying the price (death on the cross). Jesus' sacrifice brought us the gift of righteousness. Jesus' obedience has qualified us to be called the righteousness of God. If Adam's disobedience made us sinners, the obedience of Jesus has made us righteous.

There is a huge misconception concerning the definition of righteousness. Most believers tend to describe righteousness as a catalogue of things that have to be done, and fulfilling those listed items creates a sense of righteousness while failure to fulfil the listed items creates a sense of unrighteousness, which is incorrect.

Our righteousness is not determined by the things we do right. Our righteousness is a product of what Jesus did for us at the cross. We are not righteous because of our right actions or behaviour but because Jesus Christ has made us righteous. Believing right in Jesus is what makes you righteous. God rewards your believe and not your behaviour.

Not until you erode your self-righteousness, God cannot unleash His righteousness that was given to you by His grace.

The Bible says by strength shall no man prevail (that speaks of your physical works or fleshly works). You can't have enough strength in the physical to prevail, but you can have enough faith to prevail. Your travails are as a result of you trying to prevail by strength. The prevailing force of a believer is tied to his belief system.

If we are to work for righteousness, we will never be worthy enough to achieve God's standard of righteousness. Our self-righteousness is like a filthy rag before God!

> *For if by one man's offence death reigned by one; much more they which receive abundance of grace and of the gift of righteousness shall reign in life by one, Jesus Christ.*
> ROMANS 5:17

Death speaks of separation! The ultimate of death is when your spirit leaves your mortal body. There is so much to death than just having your immortal self separated from your mortal self. There is spiritual death, which means separation from God and his glory (goodness, kindness, mercy, favour, long-suffering, etc.).

Adam experienced this separation and fell short of God's glory. As a result, death consequences reigned by him. In the realm of the spirit, there is no vacuum. When there is any removal, there must be a replacement. In Adam, we were dead from God and eventually became dead in sin. Which brought death consequences such as sickness, disease, failure, retrogression, poverty, marital failure, academic failure, disappointment, etc.

> *And you hath he quickened, who were dead in trespasses and sins;*
>
> *Wherein in time past ye walked according to the course of this world, according to the prince of the air, the spirit that now worketh in the children of disobedience.*
>
> *Among whom also we all had our conversation in times past in the lust of our flesh, fulfilling the desires of the flesh and of the mind; and were by nature the children of wrath, even as others.*
> EPHESIANS 2:1-3

For there to be a reigning, there must be a thing, person or a world to rule over. Death and its consequences had rulership over the souls of men by the offence of Adam.

GRACE: *God's Reliable Abundance by Christ's Effort.*

It is abundance of grace made available by God for us to reign in life now. Hallelujah!

We have received abundance of grace and its by-product that is the gift of righteousness. For us to reign in this life through Jesus Christ. God's glory that was lost in Adam was restored in Jesus Christ. Glory speaks of God's goodness, kindness, mercy, favour, beauty, long-suffering, etc. God's glory is an exhaustible part of God. It speaks of His personality and nature. God's glory is God's fullness. In His glory, you find His grace; by His grace, you have the gift of righteousness.

In abundance of grace, which we have received in Christ, there is a large quantity of God's righteousness and unmerited favour released to mankind. It can also be called unlimited grace.

A gift is a something given wholeheartedly to someone, without a request for payment. It can also be defined as a present. Righteousness is a gift from God. Righteousness means right-standing before God. You don't pay to receive it. You don't need any qualification to receive a gift. Worthy of note is that righteous living is your responsibility. When you are given a gift, it is expected that you use it. In the natural, when you give out a gift, you always long to see that the recipient has used it.

What God gives to you has an expectation tag on it. The gift of righteousness is expected to produce results. You are to reign in this life. All that is required for you to reign has been made available. It's time for you to rule your world, the devil and sin. Don't allow the lust of the flesh and all oppression of the devil to have dominion over you. You are to dominate now in Christ Jesus.

TWO NOTABLE KINDS OF RIGHTEOUSNESS

1. RIGHT- STANDING BEFORE GOD:

Referred to as imputed righteousness, the goodness of God's character automatically became ours in Christ Jesus through faith. It is the gift of righteousness, which is a by-product of grace that was imputed (credited to our account) when we subscribed to the Lordship of Christ in faith.

> ***And the scripture was fulfilled which saith, Abraham believed God, and it was imputed unto him for righteousness; and he was called the friend of God.***
> JAMES 2:23

Abraham received credit for total dependency on God and not on his works (self-righteousness). This credit was righteousness. Abraham did not deserve to be credited looking at his works. He was not perfect but believing right made him perfect before God. He had flaws, he slept with Hagar a maiden and had a child out of wedlock. Abraham believed God and automatically became righteous. God is interested in crediting the accounts of those, who will put their good works and sins aside. Thereby depending on God's righteousness to be righteous.

Total dependency on God's grace does not only brings salvation, forgiveness of sins but also put on us the garment of righteousness. Which makes us accepted in the sight of God. This righteousness makes you qualify to stand before God without a sense of guilt.

In the natural, you will agree with me that when you pay money into your account, your account is said to be credited and in the same vein, when somebody pays money into your account, your account is credited. If you subscribed for an alert, you would receive the indicator on your phone. This is synonymous to what God did for you by sending Jesus Christ to die for you. On the cross, Christ credited your account with righteousness and God has been sending you alerts. "Hey Dear, your account is loaded; it's full of righteousness." He gives you an alert by sending a preacher to tell you this mystery, through His word and by the agency of the Holy Spirit. Saying; you did not work for it, I gave it to you, just believe and withdraw it. Your faith is your withdrawal's slip. The well of righteousness was opened by Christ's sacrifice.

Do you keep wondering, how could righteousness be paid into my account without me working for it? How could I be made righteous without works? How about my sins? My friend, let me tell you. The truth is if you believe that Jesus was made sin without sinning. Then you can be made righteous without your righteous works. Jesus was condemned a sinner on the cross without committing a sin because He took your place. Now you have taken His place in righteousness.

But to him that worketh not, but believeth on him that justifieth the ungodly, his faith is counted for righteousness.

Even as David also describeth the blessedness of the man, unto whom God imputeth righteousness without works.
Romans 4:5-6

God imputes righteousness without works. It is your belief in His imputed righteousness that justifies you. Not your works. You don't need works to be justified. Just believe on him that justifieth the ungodly. It is the justifier that makes the ungodly justified.

2. RIGHTEOUS LIVING:

Imparted righteousness, in which God imparts to us his righteous nature, is made manifest by the enabling power of the Holy Spirit. God's desire is for us to express our righteous nature or live a righteous life. God did not only impute His righteousness to us, but also imparted to us what it takes to live a righteous life.

In God's grace, there is an empowerment for us to live righteously. In this kind of righteousness is holiness in character and conduct. It is manifesting Jesus' life through your life. With this empowerment that comes with God's grace, you can live a holy life. The Holy Spirit is an embodiment of this power; He places in your spirit what it takes to dominate the flesh.

There is a continuous war between your spirit and the flesh. But there is a continuous empowerment from the Holy Spirit that causes your spirit always to emerge a victor. That's why walking after the Spirit is the highway to living righteously.

And ye know that he was manifested to take away our sins; and in him is no sin.

Whosoever abideth in him sinneth not: whosoever sinneth hath not seen him, neither known him.

Little children, let no man deceive you: he that doeth righteousness is righteous, even as he is righteous.
1 JOHN 3:5-7

One of the reasons Jesus died on the cross was to take away your sins and to make you righteous just as He is righteous. Your righteousness transcends beyond just standing before God as one that has never sinned, but also standing before men and expressing God's nature that was given to you. If you are in Christ Jesus, you are not meant to sin. To sin in Christ means you have not fully experienced Him. Don't be deceived, sin is sin, whether big or small. Become a practitioner of righteousness, there is grace for you to live right. He that practices righteousness is righteous, just as Jesus is righteous.

For instance, in the natural, you were penniless, wretched and miserable. You met a wealthy man who took you home, cleaned you up and put you in an estate with everything at your disposal. The only demand of this rich man was that you should take good care of yourself and always look good. In other words, he expects you to assume the state he has placed you. Appear like one who is wealthy. What do you do? Knowing fully well that you did not work for all you received from the rich man, that it was his hard earned wealth, you honoured his request because of all that he had done for you. It was a small matter for you in light of all that had been freely given to you.

Even if you were born poor, even if poverty runs through your veins, practicing as the wealthy man you have become should not be a problem. You have to learn to look good. Is it the rich man's responsibility to teach you how to behave like one that is rich? No!

In like manner, God has made you rich in righteousness. You are established in righteousness through Jesus' obedience on the cross. So it is not His duty to live it out for you. It's your responsibility. God has given to you the Spirit of Grace for you to live a righteous life.

The totality of your living as a Christian should be spent by following the leading of the Holy Spirit. Walk in the Spirit. This kind of righteousness is evident for all to see. It is seen in your conduct, attitude, and in all you do. Let Christ be seen in you and through you.

God's uttermost desire is to see you reign in this life, with the abundance grace and the gift of righteousness that you have received.

Spiritual walk is the only way to walk out on the devil and all the sins that easily beset us.

> *...that they might be called trees of righteousness, the planting of the Lord, that he might be glorified.*
> ISAIAH 61:3

Jesus has made you a tree of righteousness. Every tree produces after its kind. Mango trees produce mango fruits. Grafted into the tree of righteousness, you are meant to produce righteous fruit. When people see your righteous fruits, they will glorify God, who has called you out of unrighteousness and has established you in righteousness. Hallelujah.

> ***For what the law could not do, in that it was weak through the flesh, God sending his own son in the likeness of sinful flesh, and for sin, condemned sin in the flesh.***
>
> ***That the righteousness of the law might be fulfilled in us, who walk not after the flesh, but after the Spirit.***
> ROMANS 8:3-4

Fulfilling the law in the flesh was impossible because the flesh was dominating and the law was powerless (weak) in controlling the flesh. Sin will not permit the flesh to obey the law.

God sent Jesus Christ in the likeness of sinful flesh and for sin, condemned sin in the flesh. We have to deal with sin because sin has the power to enslave us. Therefore, sin was condemned in Christ's body on the cross, so that you would be free from condemnation. Since sinners are condemned, Jesus assumed the position of a sinner so He could be condemned for all who have sinned.

Jesus came in the form of flesh to stand in the place of our crime. So instead of us been sentenced, He was convicted in our place. Instead of you being crucified, He was crucified in your place. Christ died on the cross to liberate us from the power of sin and death. Jesus sacrificed His own life to make us righteous. Your physical flesh is always in combat with your spirit man. So the stronger your spirit man, which perpetually walks with the Holy Spirit (the Spirit of Grace, by which you were saved and sealed), the weaker your flesh becomes in luring you into sin.

The law was the standard of righteousness while grace is the source of righteousness. Jesus has made you righteous; you are to live righteously. It's your responsibility. God's nature was released to your spirit and a walk after the Spirit makes you manifestly righteous. You can't change nature. Your sins do not change God's nature of righteousness in you. They only stain your new nature. Go back to God in prayers, ask for forgiveness. He will forgive you, and the Holy Spirit will clean you up. Then you keep on walking in the Spirit of Grace, who empowers you to live righteously. Hallelujah.

John: That was powerful.

Sam: Glory to God. Hope you were blessed?

John: I was tremendously blessed.

Sam: I'm glad to hear that you were blessed. I will share more on grace in our next meeting.

Take home prayer point: Lord I thank you for your grace, thank you for giving me the gift of righteousness without my works. Thank you for the impartation of righteousness into my spirit man. I receive grace to bear fruits of righteousness as expected in Jesus mighty name. Amen.

PRE-CHAPTER CONVERSATION

John: I have been blessed so far, and I am experiencing the wonders of God's grace already.

Sam: That's good to know. Let me give a testimony of how I was empowered by grace. The grace of God has helped me in so many ways. I am bold to say I am a product of grace. This is because if not for God's grace, I don't know where I would have been now. I will just briefly give a testimony regarding how God empowered me by grace to win the war against sin. I love God and His house. I was born again, went to church, was committed to service, but still I had issue with sin.

Just like Paul said in **Romans 7:22-23,**

> *I delight in the law of God after the inward man, but still there is another part of me that is warring against the law of my mind and bringing me into captivity to the law of sin which is in my members (paraphrased).*

I desired to break out of it, but I found myself doing it. After several fruitless efforts to break out on my own, I started applying the power of God's grace. I started fasting and prayers. I meditated on the Word of Grace and cried out to God to help me and told Him that I wanted to be free so I can serve Him more effectively. Glory to God I have been set free. I have been empowered against sin. The Word of God has shaped my thought life. If you are experiencing any oppression, your freedom is guaranteed in God's grace. You are free from every manipulation of the devil in Jesus name. Amen! You can be set free from any sin. Just take it to God. That mountain you are facing might be bigger than you, but can never be bigger than God. Seek God's grace and you will see God's power at work in your life. The sin you don't frown at can drown you. This empowerment is not for you to win the war against sin only, but to dominate in all areas of your life.

In the next chapter, you will learn about the empowerment of grace, and you will be empowered to win in all areas of your life, in Jesus name.

CHAPTER FOUR

THE EMPOWERMENT OF GRACE

And he said unto me, my grace is sufficient for thee; for my strength is made perfect in weakness.

Most gladly therefore will I rather glory in my infirmities that the power of Christ may rest upon me.

2 CORINTHIANS 12:9

God's grace speaks of His strength been made perfect in your weakness. Paul said, "I celebrate, I make known my weakness so that the power (grace) of Christ may rest upon me." (Paraphrased, of course). God's strength made perfect in human weakness is grace. When you are weak, His grace strengthens you. In human capacity, you are helpless, hopeless and weak. Grace is what strengthens your human ability to assume a super-human state, thereby making capable you do the impossible in the natural world. Grace is God's enabling strength in your inner man to do things beyond your human strength. It's a supernatural empowerment, bestowed on your spirit through the Holy Spirit.

THE EMPOWERMENT OF GRACE

Strength and power go with God's grace and make you act supernaturally in the natural. It is called *enabling grace*. In other words, there is power beyond human strength to perpetually overcome sin. Grace is a resister to sin and the capability to live the life of Christ on earth. As he is, so are we. What Jesus did while on earth, we are also able to do, and even greater works. This is made possible by His grace.

For this enabling grace to be functional in our lives, we must recognise our weaknesses and rely on His grace. Total dependency on God's grace makes us overcomers. The key to acquiring supernatural empowerment of grace is absolute reliance on His ability.

> *For whatsoever is born of God overcometh the world; and this is the victory that overcometh the world even our faith.*
> 1 JOHN 5:4

God begot you by grace and within this grace lies an overcomer's ability for you to overcome the world. But for you to emerge a victor, you need faith. Grace to overcome has been made available, but your belief and faith give you access. God's grace saved you from sin and also empowered you to live above sin. Grace breaks the power of sin. Sin is powerful; God knew how powerful it would be. That's why He made provision with His grace for you to overcome sin. Grace is for your dominion on earth.

You are saved by grace and empowered by same to live the Christ life. Know that in your human strength, you are weak and susceptible to sin. But in God's grace, there is much strength to withstand sin. Satan's intention was to erase us, but by grace Jesus came to raise us. Now we have been raised above sin.

> *For sin shall not have dominion over you; for ye are not under the law but under grace.*
> ROMANS 6:14

You are under grace now. Sin is not supposed to have dominion over you again, because in grace, there is an empowerment that dominates sin. This grace enables a believer for exploits, which are bold or heroic achievements. Grace calls you for great exploits.

Human strength and willpower are limited, but grace is unlimited. Your willpower can resist sin to an extent. Your human strength can do combat with the lust of the flesh for some time, but grace gives a long-lasting resistance. If you are truly born again, you have a natural distaste for sin. It is called grace. Grace is there for you to stand strong. You need to grow in the grace of God wherein you stand. As we go on in this book, you will learn how to grow in grace. Grace is reliable because God is dependable. You can always rely on God to help you, especially when you can't help yourself.

Grace is opposite of the law. The law was established in the Old Testament to point sinners to the need for a Saviour to take away their sins. Sin shall not have dominion over you; for you are not under the law. The law implies that sin is capable of having dominion over you. The law gives sin the power to prevail. The prevalence of sin today is a function of man, trying to keep the law by strength. The more you try to keep the law, the more sin abounds. That is because you can't be perfect enough to keep all the law. You need grace.

> ***For whosoever shall keep the whole law,***
> ***and yet offend in one point, he is guilty of all.***
> JAMES 2:10

If you are to keep the law, you must be ready to keep it all, because a slight mistake in keeping the law is the same as failure in keeping all the law. A single point off track means you are guilty of all. Stop looking at the Law of Moses for self-performance, effort and perfection. Start looking unto Jesus, the author and finisher of your faith who has fulfilled the law on your behalf and has made you law-free. Your holiness, righteousness and performance should no longer be a product of self-efforts but Jesus' effort.

> ***Think not that I am come to destroy the law, or the prophets:***
> ***I am not come to destroy, but to fulfil.***
> MATTHEW 5:17

Jesus fulfilled the law by living without sin. That means He never failed a point of the law. He was able to totally keep the law. You couldn't have been able to do that.

He is all you need now to live righteously. His grace has set you free from the bondage of the law and sets you on a platform where you live a righteous life through faith. Your works can never please God, only your faith can, your faith in Jesus' finished work on the cross! God is ever pleased with people who by faith in the finished work of Christ are made perfect, righteous and holy. However, God is not please with those who depend on what they can offer in their human capacities to keep the law. The law reveals sin and strengthens it to prevail over you, while Grace reveals sin and gives you the ability to withstand it.

God's grace is full of potent power to make overcomers; your faith determines its effects. Have faith in God all you graceful and powerful people of God. Desist from your own works and rest in His works. The victory Jesus won for you gives you the ability to overcome, but your faith is what brings about the manifestation.

> ***But unto them which are called, both Jews and Greeks,***
> ***Christ the power of God, and the wisdom of God.***
> 1 CORINTHIANS 1:24

Jesus Christ is the power of God and the wisdom of God. God's plan for man's redemption is a display of His power and wisdom. The devil did not know this plan earlier. Had he known he would not have allowed Jesus to be crucified. I believe he would have volunteered to be Jesus' bodyguard to avoid Him being crucified!

> *⁶ Yet we do speak wisdom among those who are mature; a wisdom, however, not of this age nor of the rulers of this age, who are passing away;*
>
> *⁷ but we speak God's wisdom in a mystery, the hidden wisdom which God predestined before the ages to our glory;*
>
> *⁸ the wisdom which none of the rulers of this age has understood; for if they had understood it they would not have crucified the Lord of glory*
>
> 1 CORINTHIANS 2:6-8

God manifested His power through the death and resurrection of Jesus Christ.

> *But as many as received him, to them gave he power to become the sons of God, even to them that believe on his name.*
>
> JOHN 1:12

Your willingness to receive Him brings into your life the power to become a son. Your Sonship is a product of the power you received when you gave your life to Jesus Christ. It was not your making; it was His ability working in you and changing your status into a son in the kingdom. That's grace at work. Glory to God!

> *And declared to be the Son of God with power, according to the Spirit of holiness, by the resurrection from the dead.*
>
> ROMANS 1:4

The death of Christ on the cross and His resurrection was a total display of power through the Holy Spirit. Jesus was manifested to be the true Messiah and Saviour of all men by the display of power through the Holy Spirit, who raised him from the dead.

> *For I am not ashamed of the Gospel of Christ; for it is the power of God unto salvation to everyone that believeth; to the Jews first, and also to the Greek.*
> ROMANS 1:16

The gospel of Christ is the power of God unto salvation. The power that was displayed at the cross is capable of bringing salvation. This same power can keep you from sinning. All you need to enjoy this great empowerment is faith. The revelation of the cross unleashes power that breaks the backbone of sin. The era of the *human race* ended with the death of Jesus Christ on the cross. While the era of *grace race* began at the cross and with His resurrection.

> *For the preaching of the cross is to them that perish, foolishness; but unto us which are saved, it is the power of God.*
> 1 CORINTHIANS 1:18

When the cross is preached, there is such power that emanates from the Gospel. This power is an enabling power of God that enables us to live the Christian life. You cannot live the Christian life independent of God's grace. When the essence of grace is made known and appreciated, sin loses its grip on your life. Sin becomes powerless. There is supernatural empowerment that comes with the grace of God and the preaching of same, that makes you live holy. Grace saves you, and you are to stand by grace also **(Romans 5:1-2)**.

Know that all you are is grace made. All you will ever be is grace determined. You need to acknowledge God's grace and maximize it in your life.

> *Wherefore let him that thinketh he standeth take heed lest he falls.*
>
> *There hath no temptation taken you, but such as is common to man. But God is faithful not to suffer you to be tempted above you are able, but will with the temptation also make a way to escape, that you may be able to bear.*
> 1 Corinthians 10:12-13

Paul speaking, he says: if you know you are on track, be careful on how you walk. Don't allow anything to bring you to a fall. There are many distractions here and there. Keep standing for Christ. Christ is looking for those that will stand irrespective of the temptation they are facing in the world.

Before you were tempted, God knew and had strategized a technique needed for you to overcome. He placed in you what I call "temptation resister." Before you are ever tempted, a way of escape has been designed, and that escape route is known as grace. There is an overcomer's ability in you that makes you able overcome sin. You need to recognize it and start utilizing it. Please pause a moment and take a good look at your previous status as an unbeliever. If you are truly born again, you will realise that there are things you use to do that you can no longer do now. In your new status as a new creature, *you are no longer comfortable with sin*. It's not you; it's the grace of God at work in you.

Know this, that there is no temptation you have faced or will ever face that is new. Somebody somewhere has experienced it or is experiencing it. And God sees all. He knows it's temporary, and it's meant to make you strong and fit. Christianity is not an escape route to a world of no temptation. It is an intake to a world of temptations where you will be tempted not by God, but by the devil. It is a world full of wars, but the good news is you are an overcomer. God has empowered you over sin, the devil and all his oppressions.

THE EMPOWERMENT OF GRACE

> ***Submit yourselves therefore to God. Resist the devil, and he will flee from you.***
> JAMES 4:7

When you submit yourself to God, the devil becomes your subject. You are no longer under his control. At this point, you have been equipped with what it takes to rule. You can now resist him and he flees. God would not ask you to resist the devil if He had not placed in you a resister to withstand him. Submitting to God is an act of faith in response to His grace. When you do this, then the devil and all his temptations can be resisted. To submit means to totally yield yourself to God. It is a total yielding of your will and emotion to God.

There is an empowerment in grace that sets us free. Grace is when human strength is ignored for power from above to prevail. Submitting to God is a sign that you realise how weak you are to help yourself. Now that you know, you can do nothing in the flesh independent of God's grace. Therefore, operate in total abandonment where you totally abandon yourself to God. You must leave all your self-efforts and yield your life to Him, who can work in you both to will and to do of His good pleasure. Absolute dependence on God is the secret to success as a Christian.

> ***For it is God which worketh in you both to will and to do of his good pleasure.***
> PHILIPPIANS 3:13

There is a supernatural power at work in you both to will and to do of His good pleasure. This power is beyond human willpower. It's a power from above. When this power resides in you, you naturally do God's will and your life becomes pleasing to Him. God's good pleasure becomes your delight. You will naturally seek to please God in everything you can. This power is made manifest in your life when you realise your incapability to do God's will or please Him in the flesh. In other words, when you see how impossible it is for you to do right without His power, when you see your deficiencies, His efficiency will be released in and through you.

Stop striving to fulfil the law to be accepted by God. Stop working hard in your physical strength to be pleasing to God. Start yielding yourself in faith to God for Him to work through you. God's power at work in you is capable of making you into who God desires you to be.

Stop *doing* to become, thereby putting yourself under legalism. Start *believing* in Jesus Christ and what He has done to become, thus hiding under grace. No amount of self-works can win God's grace. It is God's prerogative to release grace on those that depend solely on him.

If you try to work for righteousness, you will not be able to achieve God's standard of righteousness. Stop thinking that you are saved, blessed and pleasing to God by your works of righteousness. Rely on the One who has the power to make you do His will and His good pleasure. God is at work in you dear valued ones! Yield yourself to Him and see the mystery of a supernatural power at work in you. The devil will no longer have power over you in the name of Jesus. I pray for you that you will have a repellent heart that will repel every thought and desire of sin in Jesus name.

Then he answered and spake unto me, saying.
This is the word of the Lord unto Zerubbabel, saying.

Not by might, nor by power, but by my Spirit, saith the Lord of host. Who are thou, O great mountain? before Zerubbabel thou shalt become a plain, and he shall bring forth the headstone thereof with shoutings, crying, Grace, grace unto it.
ZACHARIAH 4:6-7

What are the mountains, habits, challenges or temptations you are facing? What are those weights that weigh down your Christian life? No matter how great your muscular strength is, you cannot make a mountain into a plain. It's not by might, nor by power but by the Spirit of Grace. The power of God is what you need to make those mountains into plains. Shout grace, grace to the mountain. Take the mountains in your life to God in prayers. His grace can bring down any mountain. Speak grace to the mountain and it will become a plain. Grace is your weapon to bring down any mountain. Mountains answer to grace, not to your muscles. Grace has conquered it all. Just speak grace to it and see the reality of its power.

> ***More over the law entered, that the offense might abound but where sin abounded, grace did much more abound.***
> ROMANS 5:20

Grace is released to overcome sin. You need to acknowledge and depend on this grace so that this power can prevail over that sin you are struggling with. No matter how enslaved you are in sin, there is something more powerful, which is the grace of God. In a world where sin abounds, more grace abounds to withstand sin.

The law came in to reveal your faults and lack of capacity. The essence of the law was to show your offenses and make you responsible for them. The law is a product of anger, but grace is a product of love. Great is the mystery of the power of grace over the power of sin. Grace delivers you from sin and also enables you to live above sin. Please note that grace and sin don't mix. You can't wallow in sin and claim to be under grace. You need to start appropriating God's grace to see your freedom from sin. Mixing faith with grace is what breaks the backbone of sin over your life. Grace destroys the power of sin Hallelujah!

> *Sin does not stop God's grace from flowing, but God's grace will stop sin.*
> Joseph Prince

John: That was powerful. It's been a glorious ride on the Word of Grace.

Sam: Yeah. See you soon as we explore more of God's grace.

Take home prayer point: Dear gracious God, I thank you for empowering me with your grace against the power of sin. I am full of grace and I overcome sin. Sin no longer has power over me, there is no stopping me in destiny fulfilment. I walk in the power of your grace in Jesus name. Amen.

PRE-CHAPTER CONVERSATION

John: Hello brother Sam. How are you doing?

Sam: Hey, I am fine and you?

John: I'm fine thanks.

Sam: It's so good to see you again. Let me continue from where I left off in our last meeting. My spiritual life took a new dimension after my encounter with the power of God's grace. It has been glorious. I have been growing from one level of grace to another. I have an intimate relationship with God and there is nothing holding me back from serving Him effectively. My service to God flows with more freshness, and I experience zeal with understanding.

John: Please can you tell me how you have grown over time and are still growing in grace?

Sam: Oh yeah! I will be glad to let you know that. I grew in God's grace through His Word, thanksgiving, humility, fasting and prayer of request, and I am still growing in grace. On earth, you need grace to succeed in all areas of life. There is no end to growing in grace.

Follow me to the next chapter, let me show you practical keys to multiply God's grace in your life.

CHAPTER FIVE

GRACE CHANNELS

But grow in grace and in the knowledge of our Lord and saviour Jesus Christ. To him be glory both now and forever. Amen.

2 PETER 3:18

Grace is in degrees. You can increase in grace. You can grow in grace, it can be increased in your life. There is no end to growing in God's grace. The more graceful you are, the more graceful you should always desire to be. When Grace stops growing, it ends in disgrace. For you to keep enjoying a graceful life, you must keep the growth process of grace going. You will always need more grace at any level you may find yourself. How can you grow in grace? There are channels through which grace can be multiplied in your life. Grace channels include: **God's Word, prayer of request, thanksgiving, fasting and humility.** Note that these channels of grace are not grace qualifiers, they are grace quantifiers. Faith is the only qualifier needed for grace to be made manifest at any level.

GOD'S WORD

And now, brethren, I commend you to God, and to the word of his grace, which is able to build you up, and to give you an inheritance among all them which are sanctified.
ACTS 20:32

The Word of God is God's grace in print. The gospel of Jesus Christ is the grace of God. The Word of God is a compendium of grace. God has placed His ability to cause change in your life in His Word. The Word of God is full of life-building materials. The beauty of a building is concealed until it is roofed, painted, glassed and completed. The beauty of God's grace in you through Christ's completed work on Calvary, is meant to be seen by all. But you have to be built by the Word of His grace. People need to see holiness, forgiveness, love, success and other attributes of grace in you. These are evidence of grace. Children of God need to show the fruits of godliness.

Grace builds you up and gives you an inheritance among the sanctified. Because of redemption, you are entitled to the abundant grace a life in Christ carries. These abundances include unmerited favour, success on every side, divine health and prosperity to name just a few. And all these are part of your inheritance in Christ Jesus. The more you discover, the more you become. Engage in a search and believe in everything you see as your entitlement in Christ. Then, automatically you will become what you believe.

Whenever you receive God's Word, you are built up to a level of grace. And from one level to another, you are changed into the same image of Christ. You cannot outgrow the grace of God on your life. Therefore, you need to grow in grace and the knowledge of our Lord Jesus Christ.

And the word was made flesh, and dwelt among us (and we beheld his glory, the glory as of the only begotten of the father), full of grace and truth.

And of his fullness have all we received and grace for grace.
John 1:14 & 16

And the Word (Jesus Christ) was made flesh. God created a body for the Word to live in and restore all men in the flesh. God is a Spirit. So Jesus Christ came down in human flesh, to set us free from the flesh. He was 100% Spirit and 100% human. He became a human being like you, and a Spirit being at the same time. What was done in the sinful flesh in Adam necessitated sinless, perfect flesh to be eradicated. That sinless, perfect flesh was Jesus, who died in your place. For sin, He was condemned to the cross. He was condemned on the Cross to deliver you from condemnation. He took your (and my) place.

Jesus is full of grace and truth. Of His fullness have we received and grace for grace. Jesus is grace personified. God poured His grace on us through Jesus Christ. Jesus is full of grace. We have received this grace in abundance. Grace and truth go hand in hand. Jesus is the Word of God made flesh. The more you learn of Him, the more of Him you become. He is full of grace and truth. Graceful people are Word labourers. Those who labour in the Word to become like Jesus Christ are not the same those who labour in human strength or are performance-driven folks. You cannot see your inheritance in Christ if you do not continually view the Word of Grace. The word you receive breaks the dominion of sin upon your life.

He said come unto me, all ye that labour and are heavy laden and I will give you rest.

Take my yoke upon you, and learn of me; for I am meek and lowly in heart; and ye shall find rest unto your souls.

> *For my yoke is easy, and my burden is light.*
> MATTHEW CHAPTER 11 VERSE 28, 29 AND 30.

The more you learn of the fullness of His grace and truth, the more grace abounds to give you rest in every area of your life that you have been struggling. He said, "Come unto me, all you that labour," (striving in the flesh to fulfil the law, struggling with habits, sin and all oppressions of the devil) "and are heavy laden," (are weary, weak and unfruitful) "and I will give," (I will make you desist from works and relax to enjoy the fruits of my finished work). Hallelujah!

By strength shall no man prevail, but by His enabling power and truth in your Spirit, you possess a prevailing force, unstoppable by the enemy. He said, "Learn of me." You are to learn of the master, full of grace and truth. Grace is not a substitute for labouring in the Word, it only makes your labour glorious.

A restful soul is a soul that has answers to every question of life; a worry-free soul; a soul that has what it needs without struggling for it. All these happen when you labour to learn of Him.

> *But by the grace of God I am what I am;*
> *and his grace which was bestowed upon me was not in vain;*
> *but I laboured more abundantly than they all; yet not I,*
> *but the grace of God which was with me.*
> 1 CORINTHIANS 15:10

"I am what I am today by the grace of God and His grace bestowed upon me was not in vain," says Paul. Paul realised that he was made who he was by God's ability working in his life (Grace). He did not stop there; he went further to say that he laboured more abundantly than them all. There is room for labour in God's Word. Grace increases in the lives of those that are committed to God's Word and work. Do you know that you can waste God's grace upon your life by completely folding your hands and doing nothing? Folding of hands and doing nothing can frustrate grace. It can make grace unproductive. The more you commit to studying, the more grace is released for a studious lifestyle and ability to live a balanced Christian life.

> *Thy word have I hid in mine heart,*
> *that I might not sin against thee.*
> PSALMS 119:11

Be committed to God's Word and the devil will be committed to running far from you. Your lack of the Word is the reason behind the mess you are experiencing. Lack of God's Word makes you vulnerable to satanic attacks and oppressions. Grace is there, but more grace is available for you to stand strong in times of challenges. Go for it!

Without a shadow of a doubt, you know in the natural there is no delivery of a baby without labour. You must labour to be able to deliver. So it is also in the spiritual, there is a labour room. In this labour room, your financial fortune, marital bliss, academic excellence, favour and above all, all-around success are birthed. The labour room is the Word of God. You labour by studying and learning. The result of your labour is made manifest for all to see. That's your baby. Just the way everybody sees the baby at the end of the labour process, that's how everybody is meant to see the manifestations of God's grace in your life at the end of every labour.

Paul said, "I laboured more abundantly than them all." In other words, he worked harder than everyone. No wonder he had such results. God's Word labourers are God's generals. There is no substitute for labour if you want to deliver. There is no easy click to enjoy God's provision without being devoted to discovering the provisions that have been made available. Jesus said, "Come and learn of me."

> *For the grace of God that bringeth salvation hath*
> *appeared to all men,*

> *Teaching us that, denying ungodliness and worldly lusts, we should live soberly, righteously, and godly, in this present world;*
>
> *Looking for that blessed hope, and the glorious appearing of the great God and our saviour Jesus Christ;*
>
> *Who gave himself for us, that he might redeem us from all iniquity, and purify unto himself a peculiar people, zealous of good works.*
> TITUS 2:11

The grace of God that brings salvation has appeared to all men. It appears to save, build, strengthen and empower men for exploits. Grace teaches. Grace teaches us how to deny ungodliness and worldly lusts. It also teaches us how to live soberly, righteously and godly in this present world. The essence of grace is to help you through life in this present world. The same power (grace) that saved you, can also make you live a holy life. Grace is a great mystery of salvation, power, deliverance and safekeeping of the saints unto the appearing of our Saviour in His second coming.

Jesus was grace personified to build a people of grace. You are powered by grace to live a balanced Christian life. Jesus brought grace and left us with a grace guide, which is the person of the Holy Spirit. He is the Spirit of Grace and truth, who is to guide us and lead us into all truth. Build a relationship with the Holy Spirit, ask Him to teach you and guide you into all truth. The grace life requires a grace guide and that's the Holy Spirit. He is your guide, helper, partner, teacher, advocate and companion. The Holy Spirit is real on earth today, just as Jesus was when He lived on earth. The only difference is that the Holy Spirit is not in a physical body form, but a Spirit. He is a person indwelling on your inside.

> *Grace and peace be multiplied unto you through the knowledge of God, and of Jesus our Lord.*
>
> *According as his divine power hath given unto us all things that pertain unto life and godliness through the knowledge of him that hath called us to glory and virtue.*
>
> 2 Peter 1:2-3

Grace multiplies through the knowledge of God and of Jesus our Lord. The more you know, the more you are empowered by grace for exploits. If you know who Christ is, what He represents, what He came to establish and what is expected of you, you will live right. The revelation of Jesus Christ makes all things that pertain to life and godliness evident in your life.

According as His divine power, grace hath given unto us all things that pertain unto life and godliness, through the knowledge of Jesus Christ who has called us to a life of glory and virtue. Acquiring knowledge of Jesus Christ releases divine power to become all Jesus represents. God has placed in His Word all things needed for our enjoyment in life and all that is needed for us to live godly lives. God has called you into an enviable life, but it is not actualisable if you lack the knowledge of who your caller is. You are called into a life of glory, honour, dignity and virtue. Let your walk with God be according to revelation in the knowledge of Him. Engage in a search to know and apply what you know in practical ways. As you do so, I see God giving you more grace for greater exploits in Jesus name.

> *For the hope which is laid up for you in heaven, whereof ye heard before in the word of the truth of the gospel.*
>
> *Which is come unto you, as it is in all the world, and bringeth forth fruit, as it doth also in you, since the day ye heard of it, and knew the grace of God in truth.*
>
> Colossians 1:5-6

The Word of Grace is the Word of the truth of the gospel. The Word of God's grace sent to you has an expectation tag on it. No wonder Paul said, "I commend you to God and to the Word of His grace, which can build you up and give you an inheritance among them that are sanctified."

Hope speaks of expectation and desire for a thing. As you hear the Word of the truth of the gospel, hope is established in heaven for you. There is an expectation in heaven for you when you hear the Word. God's earnest expectation is that, as you hear the word of truth, you do what you hear. The Word of God is a conveyor of truth and grace. It is the truth you know that establishes you in life.

God's desire in heaven is to see you bring forth fruit as you hear His Word. The divine Word is sent to you to make you a fruitful vine. God's Word carries productivity. As you hear His Word, you are to produce results. There is an expectation stored in heaven for you. When God's Word comes to you, what do you do with it? Grace increases in an environment where there are Word-doers. Doing God's Word is an application for more grace. Word practitioners are graceful people. Put to work the knowledge you have acquired. Do the Word, practice what God says. The fruits of godliness should be seen in you. The Word of Grace already has the power to make you. Your role is to align yourself to be made by it. This is possible by practically positioning yourself to act on every Word of God you hear to produce results. The grace life is all about productivity. Stop claiming to be under grace while you are still living in sin. That's procuring disgrace without knowing. Start engaging God's Word for productivity to maximize the grace life.

> ***What shall we say then? Shall we continue in sin,***
> ***that grace may abound.***
> ROMANS 6:1

Your acts of ungodliness are not justifiable under grace. Why? Because what it takes to live a holy life is available by the grace of God. Don't perpetually live in sin and expect grace to abound. There is a great difference between the practice of willful sin, and the failure which can occur in a moment of weakness. If you are truly committed to righteousness, such failures bring you quickly to repentance and sorrow for your sin. You will always want to get it right with your heavenly Father as soon as possible.

Whenever a pig falls in a mud-hole, it lays there and enjoys itself. It will return to the same dirty place whenever it can. If a sheep slips into a mud-hole, it will try it's best to quickly climb its way out and avoid the place in the future. Continuing in sin is an abuse of God's grace. The Word of Grace can build you up.

PRAYER OF REQUEST

__Let us therefore come boldly unto the throne of grace, that we may obtain mercy and find grace to help in time of need.__
Hebrews 4:16

Prayer of request for more grace is a non-negotiable requirement to multiply grace in your life. In the place of prayers, grace is released to stand in times of trials and temptations. You are required to come boldly to the throne of grace (a throne where all grace abounds), that you might take mercy and find grace to help in time of need. God is the source of grace and He is a reliable source. You can request grace at any time, He is ever ready and willing to unleash His grace on the needy. You must be in need before grace can be supplied. Your need for grace is what triggers supply. You get grace by praying and seeking God. As a Christian in this world, there will always be a time when you need help, a time you when are helpless in your strength. You can be stranded in your willpower, but you can't afford to be stranded of God's power. Go to God in prayers for grace to help. Your help is from God. Supernatural strength is bestowed on you over every harassment of the devil in the place of prayer. Grace to stand, fight and overcome sin is released when you pray. The prayer room is the grace generator room where Grace is generated to perpetually live a holy life. *To be prayerless is to be defenceless against the devil* in battle. The Spirit of Grace (the Holy Spirit) has been waiting to see your desire for empowerment. He is your helper. What is the use of a helper if not to help you when you are in need?

Mercy is obtainable. If you have messed up, you have a reliable source where you can obtain mercy to clean up your mess and forge ahead. Grace is findable, it is abundant in the throne of grace. Go for it if you are needy. Request for grace to help you in that difficult situation of your life. There must be a seeking for you to find. It's time you start seeking grace.

> ***Watch and pray, that ye enter not into temptation;***
> ***the Spirit indeed is willing, but the flesh is weak.***
> MATTHEW 26:41

Jesus admonished the disciples to watch and pray to avoid falling into temptation. Prayerfulness brings you into a realm of dominion over sin and all temptation of the devil. In the place of prayer, your spirit is invigorated with supernatural power to overcome the flesh in times of battles. Your flesh is always weak when it comes to resisting temptations. Flesh will always want to respond to fleshly desires, but thank God for your spirit man, which in a perpetual walk with the Spirit of Grace will always conquer the flesh and its lust thereof.

When you pray, you strengthen your spirit man. When your spirit man is strengthened, your flesh is strengthened and ultimately avoids wrongdoing. Your prayer life pays attention to building spiritual capacity, which in turn reflects in your physical resistance to temptation. A prayerful believer eventually becomes a graceful saint. Prayer releases supernatural strength to withstand sin and all oppressions of the devil.

The more prayerful you become, the more strengthened your spirit man becomes. When there is a spiritual willingness to do what is right and a fleshly willingness to do what is wrong, it implies that the devil is at work in your flesh to lure you into sin. For you to keep the spiritual willingness stronger, you need to engage in prayers. You can become a champion if you can be a prayer warrior. There is a continual war between your spirit and your flesh (body). It's time to engage in spiritual warfare. Engage in warfare with the mindset of a victor. You are a victor because of what Jesus did for you. When you realise how victorious you are and take advantage of your victory in Christ Jesus, the devil will stay clear from you. Victory is your portion in the name of Jesus.

> *Likewise the Spirit helpeth our infirmities;*
> *for as we know not what we should pray for as we ought;*
> *but the Spirit itself maketh intercession for us with*
> *groanings which cannot be uttered.*
>
> *And he that searcheth the hearts knoweth what is the mind*
> *of the Spirit, because he maketh intercession for the saints*
> *according to the will of God.*
> ROMANS 8:26-27

Another supernatural way to keep your spirit man supernaturally empowered is by praying in the Spirit. The Spirit of Grace (The Holy Spirit) helps our weaknesses when we pray in the Holy Ghost. The Spirit of Grace knows your spiritual capacity and He imparts grace into your spirit man according to the measure required. He knows God's will for you and prays for you in that manner. When you are faced with the mystery of iniquity, engage in the mystery of righteousness through the mystery of tongues speaking. When your spiritual communication is not comprehendible by the devil, he becomes confused and thus, gives up.

> *But ye, beloved, building up yourself on your most holy faith*
> *praying in the Holy Ghost.*
> JUDE 1:20

Supernatural strength is released when you pray in the Holy Ghost. To maintain your most holy faith, you need to engage in praying in the Holy Ghost. The Holy Spirit is the Spirit of holiness. He imparts holiness to your faith. Therefore, you need to pray in tongues for your faith to assume its most holy state.

Speaking in tongues fortifies and energizes your spirit man to stand strong in faith. I see the Spirit of Grace imparting you with more grace to stand against the wiles of the devil in Jesus name.

THANKSGIVING

Now thanks be unto God, which always causeth us to triumph in Christ, and maketh manifest the savor of his knowledge by us in every place.
2 CORINTHIANS 2:14

What you celebrate always appreciates. If you recognize God's grace at work in you and celebrate it, it will eventually multiply. You are triumphing in Christ by God's grace, not by your cleverness, expertise, smart works or deeds of righteousness. You are triumphing because God has ordained your triumph in Christ Jesus. Gratitude for grace enjoyed is an application for more grace. You can't be grateful and not enjoy a continuous flow of grace. Grace flows in the direction of its celebrants. Grace talkers are grace takers. You can't talk of God's grace and not take more grace.

When you see yourself accomplishing things beyond your human capacity, know that grace is at work. Celebrate it and you will enjoy more of it. Most people have stopped growing in grace because they have celebrated self-efforts for all their accomplishments.

Grace is what makes your efforts glorious. If you want to enjoy more grace, don't ever think you are commanding results because of what you are putting in, it is because of what He is putting in. Your overall success in life is a product of God's grace. Celebrate it and your grace life will appreciate.

> *And such trust have we through Christ to God-ward.*
>
> *Not that we are sufficient of ourselves,*
> *but our sufficiency is of God.*
> 2 CORINTHIANS 3:4-5

We have confidence through Jesus Christ to God. We can come boldly to God through Jesus Christ. Not that we are full of skills, strength or capabilities, to claim anything of self-efforts, but our sufficiency is of God. Paul recognised the limitations of the human strength and totally depended on God's grace. When you know how weak you are in your human strength, you will learn to depend on the strong and mighty God. God's sufficiency is our sufficiency. Great men are engraced men. Your greatness in life is a product of grace. Start thanking God for His grace that has brought you thus far, and for more of the same to keep you in the race till you get to the finish line. When you realise that your sufficiency is of God, His grace becomes sufficient for you to become efficient in all you do in life.

> *And I heard a loud voice saying in heaven, Now is come*
> *salvation, and strength, and the kingdom of our God,*
> *and the power of his Christ; for the accuser of our brethren is*
> *cast down, which accused them before our God day and night.*
>
> *They overcame him by the blood of the lamb,*
> *and by the word of their testimony, and they loved*
> *not their lives unto the death.*
> REVELATION 12:10-11

Grace has appeared to all men by the power of Jesus Christ. This grace has brought salvation, strength and supernatural empowerment for you to live this Christian life. There is the accuser of the brethren (Satan), who was cast down from heaven together with his angels that rebelled against God. They (Christians) overcame him (devil) by the blood of the Lamb and by the word of their testimony. The blood of the Lamb represents the grace of God, which was demonstrated through the sinless blood of Jesus, to make us saints in Him. The devil seeks to accuse you before God as a sinner but there is a new reality for your new personality. This new reality is made manifest in your life by acknowledgement and celebration of it. If you have made a mistake or you have sinned, it does not make you a sinner. The devil accuses you to bring you into self-condemnation. Know your identity and repent of your sin and continue in the newness of life that God has given you.

What are the things you need to acknowledge and thank God for? You need to be thankful to God for making you righteous in Christ Jesus. You are a saint now, no longer a sinner because you were a sinner that was saved by grace. Celebrate God for His love toward you. You are empowered with new life in Christ. You are a new creature; you are no longer who you used to be. Your new identity in Christ is your word of testimony. Thank Him for His goodness towards you.

Your attitude of thanksgiving is an act of faith which correlates with what Jesus did for you on the cross to bring about its manifestations in your life. Jesus has done all there is to do already. Your part is to mix faith with what He has done, to practically experience it in your life. Celebrating your new reality in Christ Jesus by faith brings to reality what He has done for you. Your victory over the devil comes when you acknowledge what He has done, celebrate it and confess it. You are an overcomer. Thank God for who you have become in Christ.

FASTING

But they that wait upon the Lord shall renew their Strength; they shall mount up with wings as eagles; they shall run, and not be weary; and they shall walk and not faint.
ISAIAH 40:31

There is a strength renewal when you fast. Fasting strengthens your spirit man against the days of battles. Fasting is a spiritual exercise that builds up a spiritual capacity in your spirit man. When you fast, you mount up with wings as eagles that enable you to soar above sin and all oppressions of the devil. There are strength and power that go with fasting that make you act supernaturally in the natural.

More grace is released for accomplishment in the place of fasting. Fasting builds spiritual stamina for spiritual battles. Fasting is one of the ways to put your flesh under control. When you fast, your spirit is energized and your flesh is subjected to the influence of your spirit man. When you make commands in the spiritual realm, the devil responds according to the weight of your spirit. Fasting is one of the ways to build a heavyweight spirit. Your spiritual weight determines your spiritual level of influence.

Is not this the fast that I have chosen? To loose the bounds of wickedness, to undo the heavy burdens, and to let the oppressed go free, and that ye break every yoke?

Then shall thy light break forth as the morning, and thine health shall spring forth speedily; thy righteousness shall go before thee; the glory of the Lord shall be thy reward.
ISAIAH 58:6 & 8

A fast is designed to dislodge the works of the wicked off your life, to take away evil burdens that have been weighing you down. Fasting sets you free from all oppressions of the wicked. There are some yokes that require fasting to break. Fasting is a spiritual responsibility that positions you to be spiritually in charge of your life. Fasting brings restoration of lost glory. Sin is more than just an act. It is a power that influences people beyond their will, causing them to commit ungodly acts. The devil enslaves people through the power of sin. They engage in doing things that they would not naturally want to do. There are some challenges, habits, or addictions you are battling with. Engage in a consecrated fast and dislodge all the spirits behind those evil habits. They are spirits and spirits are to be handled spiritually. Take responsibility if you want freedom. There are spiritual demonic forces at work that need spiritual supernatural force to let you go. You need to generate enough power required for you to kick them out, and that power is acquirable in the place of fasting.

> *And when he was come into the house, his disciples asked him privately, why could not we cast him out?*
>
> *And he said unto them, this kind can come forth by nothing, but by prayer and fasting.*
> MARK 9:28-29

The disciples asked Jesus why they could not cast out the demon. Jesus explained that some demons come forth only by prayer and fasting. There are certain demonic oppositions, oppressions and manipulations that require certain spiritual exercise to be kicked off. You may have prayed and have given up on that issue. Don't give up, it's not God's plan for you to be under that oppression. Engage in fasting and prayer and see that situation turn around into a testimony. Some answers come by prayer, while some require fasting and prayers.

> *For we wrestle not against flesh and blood, but against principalities, against powers, against the rulers of the darkness of this world, against spiritual wickedness in high places.*
> EPHESIANS 6:12

What was done in the spiritual realm can only be undone in the spiritual realm. Engage in spiritual warfare to clear off every demonic harassment upon your life.

Fasting is one of the spiritual exercises that builds your spiritual muscles to withstand the devil in any spiritual battle. Go and enforce your victory over that situation. You have been declared a victor by what

Christ did for you. Until you show the devil the way out of your life, he will still be there.

HUMILITY

But he giveth more grace. Wherefore he saith,
God resisteth the proud, but giveth grace unto the humble.
JAMES 4:6-7

God resists the proud and empowers the humble. God creates resistance to the proud and gives more grace to the humble.

The worst enemy of God's grace is pride. Pride brings self-centeredness, self-consciousness, and self-acknowledgement. Pride has a central focus on self. *When you are prideful, you will be graceless.* Humble yourself before God. Be ready to admit your faults and submit to God, thereby receiving more grace. See yourself as one that is helpless and in need of help from God. Humility is not denying your strength, but admitting your weakness. Humble people recognise, acknowledge and admit that they are weak. Allowing God to become your strength in your weakness is humility.

....for without me ye can do nothing.
JOHN 15:5

You must realise that without Jesus, you can do nothing. You must realise that you are weak without Him. Know that those challenges, habits or addictions are unstoppable by your own strength. You need to be honest about your weakness. Honesty before God creates total dependency on Him.

The Pharisee stood and prayed thus with himself,
God, I thank thee, that I am not as other men are,
extortioners, unjust, adulterers, or even as this publican.

> *I fast twice in the week, I give tithes of all that I possess.*
>
> *And the Publican, standing afar off, would not lift up so much as his eyes, unto heaven, but smote upon his breast, saying God be merciful to me a sinner.*
>
> *I tell you, this man went down to his house justified rather than the other. For everyone that exalteth himself shall be abased; and he that humbleth himself shall be exalted.*
> LUKE 18:11-14

The Pharisee had no acknowledgement for his wrong doings. Instead, he saw faults in others. He saw himself as perfect and law-abiding. Jesus said it was the humble publican that went home justified. God's grace is abundant on behalf of sinners who humbly acknowledge their deficiency and totally depend on His grace for forgiveness and salvation. Grace is God's power in human weakness. When you admit your weakness, God will exhibit His grace through your life. Learn to lean on His grace. It takes humility to receive the grace of God. If you don't appear helpless before God, you can't receive grace to help in time of need.

God is not looking for self-made superstars; He is looking for those He can make superstars. He is not interested in people who don't need Him because they feel they are made already. He is interested in qualifying the unqualified. Humble yourself before God and enjoy abundant grace.

> *For this thing I besought the Lord thrice, that it might depart from me*
>
> *And he said unto me, my grace is sufficient for thee: for my strength is made perfect in weakness. Most gladly therefore will I rather glory in my infirmities that the power of Christ may rest upon me.*
> 1 CORINTHIANS 12:8-10

God's power is made perfect in human weakness. Paul said that he would gladly boast of his weakness before God, so that His power can rest upon him. One of the ways to prove your humility to God is by acknowledging your weakness. You are powerless in your strength to live this Christian life. You need to rely on God's power to live a balanced Christian life. Humility is a platform upon which grace multiplies. When you are humble, you are endowed with more grace. Pride is an enemy of grace. Humility is a friend of God's grace. It attracts grace. The more humble you are, the more grace you carry. Humble yourself if you want to multiply in the grace of God. Remember God opposes the proud and releases grace to the humble.

John: That was powerful. Though it's a long one, it's filled with practical steps to place a demand on more grace. That word so blessed me.

Sam: Yeah. I'm happy you learnt something and you were blessed. Looking forward to seeing you as we go deeper in our next discussion.

Take home prayer point: Father, I thank you for your grace at work in my life. Thank you for showing me ways to grow in your grace. I pray for grace to put to work all I have learnt and to consciously do what I need to do to ensure I grow more in grace.

PRE-CHAPTER CONVERSATION

Sam: Hello, how have you been? Putting to work what you have learnt so far?

John: Fine, thanks. Oh yeah. I have started applying what I have learnt.

Sam: That's good to know. Let me show you more on how grace empowers for kingdom service. Grace is multi-diversified in nature. It can make you do what you cannot naturally do by human strength. It empowers the weak with strength. It gives you supernatural strength to serve God effectively at any level. You might be worried about that call or that new assignment given to you. The cure to your worries is the strength that comes with God's grace for the assignment. Whatever God has called you to do, He has supernaturally empowered you for it. Some people might be wondering how you are getting the job done. The reason is that you don't look like it, but a divine force is propelling you and energizing you to get the job done. That force is grace. It is God's power at work in you. Whatever you find yourself doing in the house of God, desire the grace of God to get it done. I have seen this grace at work in my service to God in His vineyard.

CHAPTER SIX

GRACE FOR SERVICE

As every man hath received the same one to another,
as good stewards of the manifold grace of God.

If any man speak, let him speak as the Oracles of God; if any
man minister, let him do it as of the ability which God giveth;
that God in all things may be glorified through Jesus Christ,
to whom be praise and dominion forever and ever. Amen.

1 PETER 4:10-11

Grace is God's ability working in your life. Every task given by God comes with grace to match. Whatever task God gives, there is always a measure of grace required for it to be accomplished. God's assignment is backed up with God's grace.

Your greatness in any assignment given to you by God is a product of His grace. God cannot give to you what you will not depend on Him to achieve. The assignment He gives to you will always need Him to be accomplished.

GRACE FOR SERVICE

Manifold here implies multi-diversified different forms or kinds. In other words, grace is many-sided. Grace is not just unmerited favour. It's far more than that. Unmerited favour is an accompanist of God's grace. It comes with God's grace. Grace stands for God's reliable abundance by Christ effort. This chapter deals with the supernatural empowerment of grace that empowers a believer to render a fruitful and successful service to God.

You are called to minister, and you can only do it by God's ability (Grace). In ministry, it is not human ability, expertise, skilfulness, smartness or cleverness that get things done. It is the power, strength and ability of God at work in us that get things done. As a minister, your caller (God) has placed in your mouth what to say. You are God's mouthpiece. He speaks through you. He has given you a message, deliver the message as an Oracle of God. He has placed in you the ability to be effective in that task He gave you. Let your ministration be according to His ability at work on your inside. You can do nothing without Him so learn to deliberately depend on Him to work through you.

Your maximum manifestation in your task is ultimately dependent on God. Recognise your source and rely on Him. Any task God gives will always need God to be fulfilled. I see your struggle in your area of assignment ends as you depend on God's grace. In Jesus name.

What He has called you for, He has equipped you for. God's ability accompanies God's assignment to any believer. Stop relying on self-abilities to bring that vision to fruition. If it is a self-ambitious mission, then you can remove God from the equation. But if it is God's vision, then you need God's power to get it done.

You may be asking, "Why did God call an unqualified person like me?" There is an answer to that question. The reason God calls the unqualified is to qualify them through His grace. God is interested in qualifying the unqualified. God called you to define His grace through you. Your life and ministry will be a definition of what grace is in Jesus name.

> *For ye see your calling, brethren, how that not many wise men after the flesh not many mighty, not many noble, are called.*
>
> *But God hath chosen the foolish things of the world to confound the wise; and God hath chosen the weak things of the world to confound the things which are mighty.*
>
> *And base things of the world, and things which are despised, hath God chosen, yea, and things which are not to bring to nought things that are.*
>
> 2 Corinthians 1:26-28

God is looking for the foolish to make wise, the weak to make strong, the despised to make renowned. God does not call the qualified but qualifies the called. Just imagine! Not many wise, not many mighty, not many noble, are called. The reason God doesn't use these people is because He wants all the glory. If He uses the wise, mighty and noble, the potentiality of them taking credits to themselves will be there. Pride will set in. By choosing the unqualified, when the results are known, the wise will think it is His wisdom at work. The mighty will think it is His strength at work. The noble will think it is His influence at work. By so doing grace will be show through. God wants His grace to be at work in you.

In the natural, we are weak emotionally and intellectually, limited and inadequate. Grace is what supernaturally makes us superhuman, thus fulfilling God's plan and purpose for our lives in a grand style. God's enabling strength is deposited in your inner man, to undertake the task.

> *Whereunto I also labour, striving according to his working, which worketh in me mightily.*
>
> Colossians 1:29

Grace does not eliminate labour; it gives beauty to your labour. Don't try to labour outside grace. Let your labour be according to His grace at work in you. Grace increases in the lives of those that are committed to God's work and Word. Paul said, "Whereunto, I also labour, but my labour is according to His power which worketh mightily in me." The meaning of "His working" in this scripture talks about His power. As much as labouring is necessary, you don't have to rely on your labour to be fruitful and successful. You are working, but still depending on His grace. Your work is unproductive without His power at work in you. You need His backing to embark on that task. If He is not backing you, things will backfire.

> **For it is God which worketh in you both**
> **to will and to do of His good pleasure.**
> PHILIPPIANS 2:13

God is the one working in you, both to fulfil His plans and desires for your life. To live a life pleasing to Him, don't take the glory if you are already operating in that capacity. Return all the glory to Him for more grace. God is working, are you ready to walk with Him? Walk in line with the workings of His grace upon your life. Receive abundance of grace to do the work of the Lord. When men see your glorious manifestations, they will know that indeed God's grace is at work in you. Glory to God!

> **And with great power gave apostles witness of the resurrection**
> **of the Lord Jesus; and great grace was upon them all.**
> ACTS 4:33

The apostles were able to effectively witness the resurrection of Jesus, according to the great power God gave them. It was God's grace that got the work done through them.

You can't be an effective witness of Jesus Christ without being engraced by Him. Your greatness in your assignment is tied to His grace.

> *Neither is there salvation in any other:*
> *for there is none other name under heaven given among men,*
> *whereby we must be saved.*
>
> *Now when they saw the boldness of Peter and John,*
> *and perceive that they were unlearned and ignorant men,*
> *they marvelled and they took knowledge of them,*
> *that they had been with Jesus.*
>
> ACTS 4:12-13

According to this scripture, the people rated Peter and John, went through their qualifications, and found out that they were unlearned and ignorant men. The people concluded that Peter and John had been with Jesus, which implies that Jesus had imparted them with such grace as He had. There was an evident rub off of Jesus' grace upon their lives. This is what grace can do. People see your imperfections and lack of qualifications and skills. But they cannot deny the proofs of His grace in your life. When they see the result, and it is not traceable to your human capabilities, then they can trace it to God. Grace is a pointer to God's involvement in that task. If it is not there, then it means self-effort is what gets the job done. When people see your results and all they see is how hard working you have been, without any trace of grace in the results you are commanding, then you need to double check if you are neglecting something of significance. Grace is a significant factor that empowers you to work and also brings about productivity for work done. Don't look down on yourself, look up to God. God is at work in you. Grace has unlimited capabilities to enable you to do what God has called you to do. Grace breeds boldness. The disciples were bold, and it was an indication that they had a supernatural backing. Grace brings courage and utterance to a minister.

> *For it is not ye that speaks,*
> *but the Spirit of your father which speaketh in you.*
>
> MATTHEW 10:20

When you stand to minister, there is a switch over of utterance. Your utterance is switched over to that of the Holy Spirit. What He says is what proceeds out of your mouth. The Spirit of God, your Father, is the Spirit of Grace. He is at work in you, speaking through you according to the measure of grace accrued to you for that task.

> ***Faithful is he that calleth you, who also will do it.***
> 1 THESSALONIANS 5:24

Faithful is your caller, who also will do what He has called you for. He called you for a purpose, and that purpose will only be actualised through you. Walk with Him and He will work through you. Have faith in God concerning His promises, He is ever faithful and will bring to pass whatever He has promised. Depend on Him to perform what He has said. Your calling is from God, and your effectiveness is guaranteed by Him also.

> ***Wherefore we receiving a kingdom which cannot be moved, let us have grace, whereby we may serve God acceptably with reverence and godly fear.***
> HEBREWS 12:28

Grace is needed for acceptable service unto God. Without grace, you can't render right service to God. If there is acceptable service, it means there is also unacceptable service. God's grace is what you need to serve God well. With grace at your disposal, you just render services to God from your heart without weariness. You don't have to be cajoled to do God's work. Serving God's interests becomes your delight. The willingness to do what pleases Him will be there. You don't struggle to serve. You can't reverence and serve God with Godly fear if you don't have the grace required to do so. Grace is all you need for acceptable stewardship.

John: That's great.

Sam: Yeah. You need grace to serve God effectively. God has given you grace to match any task He gives to you. See you soon, for the next topic of discussion.

Take home prayer point: Father, I thank you for your supernatural power at work. Thank you for empowering me by your grace to serve you effectively. Without you, I can do nothing. Please grant me more grace to render my service unto you without weariness in Jesus name. Amen.

PRE-CHAPTER CONVERSATION

Sam: Welcome to today's discussion. I will be showing you the place of the Holy Spirit in ensuring you live a graceful life.

John: Ok, thanks.

Sam: The Holy Spirit is the Spirit of Grace. Without Him, you can do nothing. He is your guardian. He watches over you. He is meant to empower you against sin and cause you to triumph over the devil in all aspects of your life. For you to win and keep winning, you need Him. God connects to your spirit man through the Holy Spirit. If your spirit man is weak, you will equally be weak in combating against sin. You need a constant walk in the Spirit to keep your connection to God alive. When you are in full connection to God and stay spiritually alive, the devil is disconnected from your life completely. No better way to live a spiritual life than with the help of the Holy Spirit. Your triumph is tied to your connection to Him. Don't take His role for granted. Walk in the Spirit.

The next chapter will reveal the Spirit of Grace, His role and how to maximize the grace He carries for you.

CHAPTER SEVEN

THE SPIRIT OF GRACE

For if we sin wilfully after that we have received the knowledge of the truth, there remaineth no more sacrifice for sins.

But a certain fearful looking of judgement and fiery indignation, which shall devour the adversaries,

He that despised Moses' law died without mercy under two or three witnesses;

Of how much sorer punishment, suppose ye, shall he be thought worthy, who hath trodden underfoot the son of God, and hath counted the blood of the covenant, where with he was sanctified, an unholy thing, and hath done despite unto the Spirit of Grace?

HEBREWS 10:26-29

THE SPIRIT OF GRACE

Under the law, there was a shadow of the reality of grace, but the substance had not yet arrived. So, sacrifices were made, that seasonally assumed the cleansing of sins. It was not possible for the blood of bulls and goats to completely eradicate sins. This necessitated the blood of Jesus Christ, that sanctified and totally eradicated sin once and for all. Jesus offered himself as the sacrifice for sin forever. Christ's death for your sin was once and forever a done deal. He died once for your past, present and future sins (Hebrews 10:10, 12 & 14).

For if we sin wilfully after that we have received the knowledge of the truth, there remaineth no more sacrifice for sins. If we kick grace aside and engage in human philosophy and perpetually live in sin, we will incur God's wrath knowing fully well that Christ cannot die twice. He has done all the sacrifice required for sins. If you deliberately decide to live in sin, it implies you have taken for granted the sacrifice He paid. Receiving the knowledge of the truth and continuing in sin makes you inexcusable before the judgement throne of God. It means you are despising what Christ did for you on the cross. Continuing in sin endangers your spirit, you have to maximize the grace of God to end your Christian race in a grand style (Hebrews 10: 28-29).

Just imagine, if he that despised Moses' law died without mercy under two or three witnesses, how much painful punishment will be given to the person that places underfoot the sacrifices of the son of God, and takes the blood of covenant that sanctified him as an unholy thing and does so despite the Spirit of Grace?

Don't neglect God's grace. God cares about how you treat the grace He has made available to you. Don't ignore grace, maximize it to the fullest. Grace is not meant only to clean your mess; it is also meant to keep you clean. If you neglect its essence, you will suffer the consequences on the last day.

You must recognise who the Spirit of Grace is and His role in your life. The Spirit of Grace is the Holy Spirit, and He helps you to live the grace life. The Holy Spirit is here to protect you, secure you and make you arrive at your destination safely. Don't frustrate His mission in your life. He guarantees your spiritual destiny. The Spirit of Grace is at your service, to always service you, strengthen you and impart you with grace. God's Spirit strengthens and empowers your spirit to be supernaturally in charge in the natural.

> *There is therefore now no condemnation to them which are in Christ Jesus, who walk not after the flesh, but after the Spirit.*
> ROMANS 8:1

There is therefore now no condemnation to you who are in Christ Jesus. But you have to be on a walk with the Spirit of Grace to ensure that your flesh does not bring you into condemnation. Spiritual walk is the only way to walk out on the devil and all the sins that easily beset us. When you walk in the Spirit, He puts in you what it takes to dominate the flesh.

God has given you the Spirit of Grace for you to live righteously in this life. Your spirit is saved when you give your life to Christ, but it's not secured because you are still in this corrupted world, except you die (where your spirit leaves your body to face its fate). As long as you are still on earth, there is still a tendency of falling into sin. Why is it still possible to sin after salvation? Because you still have a sinful nature (body) which you have crucified with Christ by faith.

> *I am crucified with Christ; nevertheless I live; yet not I, but Christ liveth in me; and the life which I now live in the flesh I live by faith of the son of God who loved me, and gave himself for me.*
> GALATIANS 2:20

The life you are living now in the flesh is by faith. You are walking by faith and walking in the Spirit to put your flesh under subjection. This Christian life is a life of faith in God's grace.

The real you (your spirit man) is completely saved at redemption, but not completely safe until you arrive at your destination (heaven). Your body (flesh) and soul are being saved, so the security of your spirit is the priority of the Spirit of Grace. You have to walk with Him. What Christ procured for you in salvation has to be secured by you. Salvation is a full package! Part of the things Christ procured for you in His salvation package is eternal life. That precious life of God in you has to be jealously secured by you through a perpetual walk in the Spirit.

> ***For to be carnally minded is death; but to be spiritually minded is life and peace.***
> ROMANS 8:6

What you set your mind on determines what your faith stands on. The best way to stop indulging in ungodly acts is to constantly have your mind fixed on godliness. Set your mind on spiritual things and your faith will stand for the right things. Carnal-mindedness brings death. Focus on walking in the Spirit. You must constantly have a spiritual perspective in life.

Death speaks about separation! The ultimate death is when your spirit leaves your mortal body. There is more to death than just having your immortal self separated from your mortal self. The death in this part of the scripture means separation from God, which brings death consequences. Some of these elements of death include poverty, sickness, diseases, disappointment, failure, retrogression, marital failure, academic failure and all oppressions of the devil. This is spiritual death. This is the death Adam experienced as a result of sin. You will agree with me that Adam did not die in the physical the minute he sinned. He died spiritually. Sin brings spiritual death. It's a separation from light to darkness. You know that there is nothing glorious about darkness. It's full of evil. Whenever you give into carnality, you pave the way for sin. Sin brings spiritual death which has many consequences other than just physical death.

Spiritual death is the separation of your spirit from God's Spirit. When God's Spirit is separated from your spirit, then your spirit is swayed by the spirit of this world which makes all manner of death consequences to manifest in your life (Ephesians 2:2). All oppressions of the devil are by-products of death. When you are spiritually alive, you are equally physically alive. No death can identify with a man that is spiritually minded. The Holy Spirit ensures that your spirit is intact, but you have a role to play. You might be asking how you play your role. Watch what you feed your mind with. No wonder the scripture says we are to be renewed in the spirit of our minds with God's Word.

There should be a continuous renewal of your mind so that it can be spiritual. Spiritualize your mind through God's Word. Build up your faith. By faith, you can begin to live a spiritual life in the physical realm with the help of the Holy Spirit, who keeps your spirit from been influenced negatively. Whatever you do in your flesh has spiritual implications. Whatever you do in your spirit has physical implications, whether positive or negative. The reason you can be saved and not been secured is that when you sin, it affects your spirit man. The sins you commit in your flesh stain your spirit. When you die in that sin, you go straight to hell. But when you repent of it, God is ever faithful and willing to forgive you and to cleanse you from all unrighteousness (1 John 1:9 & Isaiah 1:18). These stains are not stains in your physical body but stains in your spirit man.

How does He cleanse you? Through the help of the Holy Spirit. The Holy Spirit relates to your Spirit. He cleanses your Spirit man and makes sure you are spotless and stainless. You are declared righteous by what Christ did. You still need the practice of righteousness to keep clean. A house that is well built, furnished and cleaned will need maintenance to keep it clean. Otherwise it becomes dirty with time, it will accumulate dust and dirt. This is because of the environment where the house is situated. An unkempt house in Nigeria is likely to be dirtier, compared to an unkempt house in the United Kingdom. This is due to differences in environmental hazards. So also, in this world there are environmental hazards which are detrimental to your redeemed spirit. This world is full of corruption. It's full of dirt capable of staining your redeemed spirit. Glory to God for creating an escape route for us in Christ Jesus (2 Peter 1:4). You need to remain saved and avoid been corrupted by the world and things in it.

You may have heard of some people who gave their lives to Christ at the point of death. They go straight to heaven because their spirits had not been corrupted before they died (been separated from their mortal bodies). No matter the amount of sins they committed, they still went to heaven because it's not the magnitude of sin, but it's effect on your spirit man that is a concern to God. God does not want your spirit man to be stained with sin. Heaven is a place filled with spotless saints who were sinners saved by grace. Christ came to the earth to ensure that every believer would be presented spotless before God. He has already died for your sins (2 Corinthians 5:21). You need to remain righteous. It's important to guide your salvation Dear valued ones! The Spirit of Grace is available to you which is made possible when you position yourself in such a way that He can reach you. The Spirit of Grace is available to make your spirit holy and spotless. After what Jesus Christ did, the Holy Spirit was sent to continue and make sure you remain saved and arrive safely in heaven. Hallelujah!

> ***This I say then, walk in the Spirit,***
> ***and ye shall not fulfil the lust of the flesh.***
> GALATIANS 5:16

The Holy Spirit is holy, and will always want to lead the believer in holiness in any given situation. Walking in the Spirit is the cure to fleshly desires by following the Holy Spirit's leading in every sphere of life. You need divine guidance. Walking in the Spirit is the secret of victory over the flesh. Walking in the Spirit puts your flesh under submission. Until you start walking deliberately in the Spirit, your flesh will still be the dictator of your life. Allow the Spirit of God, not your flesh to drive your life.

> *And you hath he quickened,*
> *who were dead in trespasses and sins;*
>
> *Wherein time past ye walked according to the course of this world, according to the prince of the power of the air, the spirit that now worketh in the children of disobedience.*
> EPHESIANS 2:1-2

You are made alive from having been dead in trespasses and sins. Christ has delivered you. In time past, while you were wallowing in sin, you had no control over your flesh. You did things that were in line with the world's pattern. The world influenced your actions. You walked according to the standard the world presented to you. That shows the power of sin. Sin is a spiritual influence that directs people against their will. The prince of the power of the air and the demonic spirit of this world is strongly behind sin and its influence on the lives of the people. That's why you see people doing things that are naturally not convenient. For example, homosexuality, lesbianism, murder, adultery and masturbation. The unsaved are totally under the influence of this demonic power. They engage in all manner of sins without knowing what they are doing. It takes God's grace to deliver them. Some try to justify their actions. The truth is they don't have justifiable reasons. Some want to stop, and they don't know what keeps taking them back. They just cannot explain it. In like manner, when a believer gives into carnality, sin sets in. This spiritual influence from the devil makes them act contrary to God's will. Therefore, spirituality is the watchword for every believer. Spirituality is the cure to carnality and ultimately the cure to sin.

There is the spirit of the world that works in the children of disobedience. We also have the Spirit of God that works in the children of obedience. He is the Spirit of Grace. He is at work in you both to will and to do of His good pleasure. Walk in the Spirit!

How do you walk in the Spirit? You walk in the Spirit by studying God's Word, meditating on the Word and acting on the Word. Always reflect on the Word with the help of the Holy Spirit and walk by what the Word says. Put your body under subjection by fasting and praying. Pray in the Holy Ghost. Let all you do to be regulated by the Spirit.

John: Wow! That was wonderful. I can depend on the help of the Holy Spirit.

Sam: Oh yeah. You can. He is absolutely reliable. He is always ready to help. He is so concerned about you wellbeing, spirit, soul and body. See you in a bit as we conclude this series in our next meeting.

John: Ok, thanks.

Take home prayer point: Father, I thank you for the wonderful role of the Spirit of Grace in my life. Give me the grace required to maximize this awesome privilege. Help me to walk in the Spirit as a way of life. Holy Spirit, come and walk in me and through me to the praise and glory of God.

PRE-CHAPTER CONVERSATION

Sam: Glory to God for the journey so far. Apart from all you have learnt about grace, there is still one glorious thing that you need to know.

John: Please! What's that?

Sam: It is the abundant life that is guaranteed by grace. This is God's very life that was released for your abundant supply of all things. The ultimate purpose of God's grace is to guarantee that you possess this life. Grace showed up on the scene for God's glory. Unmerited favour, divine health, success, prosperity, breakthrough and increase on every side are all classified under God's abundant life. This is what you can call *exceeding grace*. It is excess in its makeup. It is inexhaustible. Whatever you need is available in abundant life. Whatever you believe and know that God can do is available in abundant life. You know that He is the God of all flesh, and there is nothing too difficult for Him to do.

God has poured out His life to you through grace, and He is watching to see if you can make the most of it through faith. I am enjoying abundant life already and will yet enjoy all it carries for me to the fullest. I pray that you enjoy abundant life and all it carries for you to the fullest in Jesus name. Amen.

I used to be sick, but since I discovered the availability of God's grace for divine health, I have not been sick for years. I have enjoyed supernatural favour. I'm still exploring the grace of God for more abundant living. All you need is to keep feeding your faith to enlarge it, to accommodate what God has in store for you. Keep discovering all that is available for you in Christ, and you will have it.

The next chapter will unfold how abundantly blessed you are in Christ.

CHAPTER EIGHT

GRACE GUARANTEES ABUNDANT LIFE

The thief cometh not, but for to steal, and to kill, and to destroy; I am come that they might have life and that they might have it more abundantly.

JOHN 10:10

Jesus came so that you might have life and have it more abundantly. Abundant life speaks of living a life to its fullest. It implies having more than enough; having all sufficiency in all things. God's plan of redemption brings life and enjoyment. God wants you to live life excessively. Within abundant life lies prosperity, divine health, success, unmerited favour, achievements and progress. Grace is an abundant package unleashed on you by God through Christ so that you can live life to the fullest. Life is not about inhalation and exhalation only. Life is about productivity. Every human being is a living being, but not every human being is a fruitful being. The life of God you possess is what makes you fruitful. Take for instance in the natural. Do you tell people that you are living before they believe you are truly living? Living is evidently seen by all. So also, abundant life should be evident in you. It is natural to live (breathing in and out), but it is supernatural to live abundantly.

> *And this is the record, that God hath given to us eternal life, and this life is in his son.*
>
> *He that hath the son hath life, and he that hath not the son of God hath not life.*
> 1 JOHN 5:11-12

God has given us eternal life through Jesus Christ. God is a God of abundance, and He has given us abundant life. Abundant life is living eternal life. You can only live life abundantly when you have Christ. Eternal life is synonymous with abundant life. Eternal life is not only futuristic; it is now and forever. It is a life you live now and forever. To live eternal life is to live abundantly on earth and in heaven. That is living without scarcity. When life becomes hard for you, that means you are living in opposition to God's plan for your life. It is your duty to keep searching for the details of the benefits of redemption. When you see them, believe them absolutely, and they will automatically become yours. The more you discover your inheritance within God's grace, the better and faster you recover from failure, retrogression, poverty, and lack of achievement.

God's life in you is what makes life glorious. If you have Christ, you are in for a glorious life. Receiving Christ brings a new order of life where you have all things in abundance. God's grace is sufficient for you to have all sufficiency in all things. God's grace guarantees abundant life. Anything God can afford is available in Christ. Salvation qualifies you for abundant life. God duplicated His life into you through Jesus Christ. You have God's kind of life in you. You represent what God stands for on His behalf. If you can't find failure in God then you can't fail in this life. If you can't find poverty in God, then you can't be poor. If you can't find sickness in God, then you can't be sick. It's time to manifest the life of God in you.

If there are such thing as characteristics of living things in the natural, there should also be characteristics of the living God in the supernatural. These characteristics are to be expressed through your life.

> *Ye are my witnesses, saith the Lord, and my servant whom I have chosen: that ye may know and believe me, and understand that I am he: before me there was no God formed, neither shall there be after me.*
> ISAIAH 43:10

You are to be evidence that God exists. We are in a world where people are seeking proof. When they see your life, it should be living proof that God is real. God is showing forth Himself through you to the world. You are His witness that He is God. All that God represents is seen in you and through you. You are a reflection of God's personality. God's glory is radiating through you. God's life and all He is has been deposited in you through Jesus Christ. Jesus Christ came to ensure that you represent God in all aspects of life. There is nothing God has that has not been released in Christ Jesus. All things are yours for the taking now!

> *He that spared not his own son, but delivered him up for us all, how shall he not with him also freely give us all things?*
> ROMANS 8:32

God did not withhold His Son but delivered Him up for us all. That action implies He is not withholding anything from us. If God can give His best (Jesus Christ), then He can bless you through Jesus Christ. Christ in you is a guarantor of a glorious future. If you have received Christ, you have received all things freely given by God. Inside Christ's redemption package lies prosperity, divine health, unmerited favour and all-around success. God did not call you to work for the blessing, His call to you was for you to discover the blessings freely given to you. You are to

GRACE GUARANTEES ABUNDANT LIFE

discover the things freely given to you in Christ. There is no enjoyment of your inheritance without discovery. God is not holding any good thing back from you. If God can give you Jesus Christ without a price tag, He can give you all things freely. You are in for unmerited favour!

> *Not rendering evil for evil, or railing for railing;*
> *but contrariwise blessing; knowing that ye are there unto*
> *called, that ye should inherit a blessing.*
> 1 PETER 3:9

You are called by God to inherit a blessing. You are called by grace to enjoy your inheritance. Your caller is responsible for your provision. He called you to enjoy your glorious inheritance in Christ. Abundant life is available and obtainable in Christ Jesus. If you are suffering, it is not because the provision God made available in Christ was called off, but because you are ignorant of the provision. What God has called you into cannot be called off because He is responsible for every word that proceeds from His mouth. God's gifts and callings are without repentance. God does not change His mind or His plan. Once you are in His plan, you are forever in His plan. Whatever He has promised you in Christ is guaranteed.

> *Blessed be the God and father of our Lord Jesus Christ,*
> *who hath blessed us with all spiritual blessings*
> *in heavenly places in Christ.*
> EPHESIANS 1:3

God has supernaturally blessed us in Christ Jesus. You are blessed with all spiritual blessings in heavenly places in Christ. All things are yours in Christ! God's blessing for you is a done deal in Christ Jesus. He is not going to bless you; He has already blessed you. All you need is your faith to mix with the discovered blessings to make them reality in your life. Your faith is your spiritual converter that converts all these spiritual blessings into physically tangible blessings. Your blessings are established in Christ Jesus.

> *For ye know the grace of our Lord Jesus Christ, that,*
> *though he was rich, yet for your sakes he became poor,*
> *that ye through his poverty might be rich.*
> 2 CORINTHIANS 8:9

Jesus was rich, but He became poor so that you could become rich. Jesus identified with your suffering so that you can identify with him in enjoyment. He identified with you in poverty so that you might identify with Him in riches. Jesus has paid the price for your riches. You are abundantly rich in Christ. Your poverty has been nailed to the Cross. His riches are your riches. What Christ did was to place you on a receiving end where you receive all the benefits of His death and resurrection on the Cross. All things are yours, Christ paid for all; your duty is to receive. Jesus Christ deliberately became poor, so that you could assume the place of His riches.

> *And God is able to make all grace abound toward you;*
> *that ye, always having all sufficiency in all things,*
> *may abound to every good work*
> 2 CORINTHIANS 9:8

God's grace is abundant towards you for abundant supply. All sufficiency in all things is evidence of abundant life. Abundant life is having all things in sufficient measure. You don't lack in the place of abundance. Jesus' sacrifice has positioned you to live in the realm of abundance. The whole essence of grace is for your repositioning. God wants you to be a blessing to your world, and you can't be a blessing if He is not capable of giving you what it takes to be a blessing. His grace has been released on you to abound unto good work.

> *Beloved, I wish above all things, that thou mayest prosper*
> *and be in health even as thy soul prospereth.*
> 3 JOHN 2

God's earnest desire for you is to see all-around prosperity in you. God's order of prosperity entails divine health, financial prosperity, spiritual prosperity and material prosperity. Those add up to abundant life! God's plan for you is for you to live life at its best. God desires to see you succeed in all spheres of life.

Jesus has identified with us in sickness so that we can enjoy divine health (Isaiah 53:5). He has identified with us in poverty so that we might be rich and prosperous.

> *The blessing of the Lord, it maketh rich,*
> *and he addeth no sorrow with it.*
> PROVERBS 10:22

God's blessings are what makes rich, not your labour. You are rich because God has blessed you. God's unmerited favour is what makes you wealthy and prosperous. Your riches in this life are products of grace. Shift your focus away from your effort and start acknowledging the blessing of the Lord upon your life. Hard work is good, but it is grace work that colours hard work for productivity. Learn to depend on your source for abundant life. Stop depending on your hard work to live life abundantly. The most frustrating thing in life is to leave your source of supply and try to depend on your own means of supply. For you to enjoy supernatural supply, you must shift your mind from your means of supply to focus on your supplier (God). Sufficiency is of the Lord, not your earnings. It's not your inputs that bring abundance, but His blessing on your input. Enlarge your faith to receive the abundant supply in Christ.

> *Labour not to be rich; cease from thine own wisdom.*
> PROVERBS 23:4

Stop struggling to be rich by your own efforts. Riches are by-products of grace. Grace is what makes rich, not manpower. The moment you understand this, you will stop depending on your hard work and start depending on His grace work through faith for abundant life. The place of work cannot be over-emphasized, but don't rely on your works for favour and abundance. Work, but focus on God for abundance. God wants to bless the work of your hand and make you a blessing to others. You have to trust Him. God wants to bless you through multi-dimensional means. In other words, He wants to favour you. You are to enjoy unmerited favour.

> *Charge them that are rich in this world, that they be not high minded, nor trust in uncertain riches, but in the living God, who giveth us richly all things to enjoy.*
> 1 Timothy 6:17

Don't be prideful. Don't trust in your labour to be rich. Remove your trust from your money. Let your pride and trust be in the living God, who always richly gives us all things we need to enjoy.

> *And he sought God in the days of Zachariah, who had understanding in the visions of God; and as long as he sought the LORD, God made him to prosper.*
> 2 Chronicles 26:5

Seeking God brings prosperity. Your prosperity is in God. God desires your relationship with Him above and before your prosperity. When you seek God first, he will prosper you.

> *But thou shalt remember the Lord thy God: for it is he that giveth thee power to get wealth, that he may establish his covenant which he sware unto thy fathers, as it is this day.*
> Deuteronomy 8:18

Wealth is gotten by God's power, not by man's power. You cannot work hard enough to qualify for it. You can only walk your way into it by seeking God first. When God becomes your primary interest, blessing you becomes His interest. You have to remember the Lord your

God to encounter His ability to make wealth. God's grace has brought you into a wealthy place. Your enjoyment is sure in Christ.

> ***Moreover*** *whom* ***he did predestinate, them he also called: and whom he called, them he also justified: and whom he justified, them he also glorified.***
> ROMANS 8:30

There is a wonderful sequence of grace that makes your life beautiful. It starts with God determining your future in Christ. He had a thought of you, even when Adam failed in His *Plan A.*, He decided a new order of plan (*Plan B*) with you in it. Then He called you by His grace, justified you by His grace and glorified you by His grace. The end product of the manifestation of God's grace upon a man's life is glorification. God wants to beautify your life (Psalm 149:4). God derives pleasure in you and desires to make your life beautiful. Abundant life is a life of beauty, colour and glory. Grace guarantees this order of life. God preordained a glorious destiny for you in Christ Jesus. He yearns to exhibit His glory to the world, and He is doing it through you.

> ***To whom God would make known what is the riches of the glory of this mystery among the Gentiles; which is Christ in you, the hope of glory***
> COLOSSIANS 1:27

Having Christ in you is your hope of glory. If not for Christ, there is no way for you to enjoy the glory of God. The crucifixion of Jesus Christ on the Cross was to restore man's lost glory. The glory man lost in the Garden of Eden due to Adam' sin has been restored in Christ. God shared His glory with man in the garden, and man had constant fellowship with Him. But sin brought man from glory to shame. God created a way to bring man back to the place of glory. Jesus is the way through which man's lost glory is totally restored. Jesus Christ is God's final word of glory, prosperity, divine health, goodness, unmerited favour, fortune, progress and success for mankind. God is not doing anything again because all that needs to be done has been done through Jesus Christ. Just withdraw all you can with the withdrawal slip of faith. God wants you to have a life full of excitement and fulfilment. You are in Christ for glorification. Take full advantage of the grace of God. Grace is your advantage to live an abundant life on earth.

John: Thanks for this glorious journey of grace. I have been tremendously blessed.

Sam: All thanks to God. I bless God for the privilege to be able to share in His grace. I am glad you were blessed. Thanks for your time and patience. God bless you richly.

Take home prayer point: Father, I thank you for your abundant life. Thank you for making me a partaker of this life by grace. I receive grace to manifest this life. Let all the abundant supply you have released in Christ Jesus be evident in my life in Jesus name. Amen.

CONCLUSION

Winning by grace is not accidental, it is deliberate. No one ever wins a battle without consciously engaging what it takes to win. Grace is what you need to win in all areas of your life, and it has been made available. It only takes personal responsibility to see it's manifestations in your life. It takes personal responsibility to place a demand on the grace of God to deliver results in everything you do.

If you want to live a result-oriented life, then engage God's grace consciously. If you wonder why you are having struggles in your Christian life, the reason is that your glorious destiny in Christ is a threat to the devil. He is working day and night to ensure you don't achieve the heights that God has designed for you. Will you let him win this battle? He is not happy seeing you born again and living a glorified life. Glory to God, who is all knowing, who knows what you are up against, and has designed a way for you to live a victorious life in spite of the attacks of the enemy. The way to victorious Christian living is by grace.

Stand strong in grace through faith. The battle line is drawn; victory has been guaranteed in Christ. You are to start enforcing your victory. Awake and start taking responsibility, don't allow anything to stop you from enjoying your glorious destiny to the fullest. God has done all there is to be done by His grace through Jesus Christ. All that needs to be done at your end is to mix faith with what He has done. The essence of faith is for you to rely on and rest in the finished work of Jesus.

You have what it takes to live an ever-winning life. As you start engaging these principles, you shall continually win in all areas of your life in Jesus name. Amen.

God bless you real good!

ABOUT THE AUTHOR

Sam Uhunoma was born and bred in Nigeria, lives in the United Kingdom, and studied Animal and Environmental Biology (Zoology) from Delta State University-Abraka. A committed member of his local church, he once held a position as the Vice President of *Royal World Campus Fellowship*, an arm of *Ever-Increasing Word of Life Ministries.* Sam was home cell leader at *Winners Chapel*-Abakaliki during his National Youth Service Corps. He is a lover of God and a product of grace.

Sam has proven with his achievements and life experiences that absolute dependency on God's grace through faith is the secret of all-around success. Today he is spreading his message of faith in God's grace to the world. He says all his achievements are traceable to God's grace at work, and he encourages others to shift focus from self to God.

THE WINNING GRACE

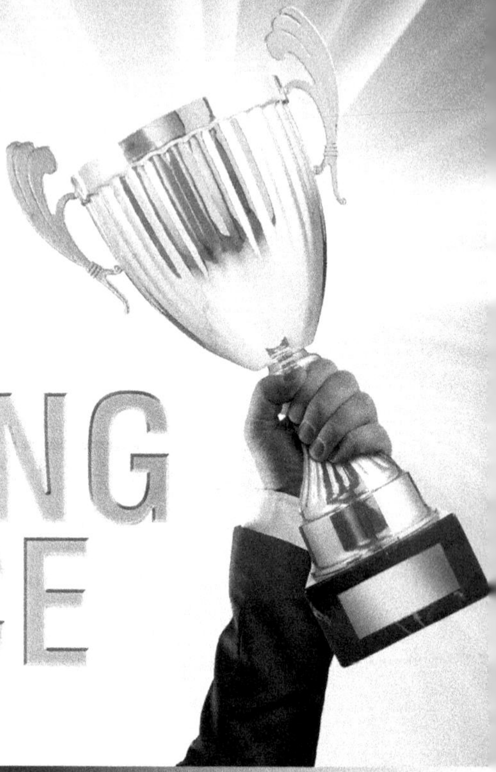

EMAIL
samuhunoma@hotmail.com

FACEBOOK
SAM UHUNOMA

TWITTER
SAM UHUNOMA

INSTAGRAM
SAMIST1

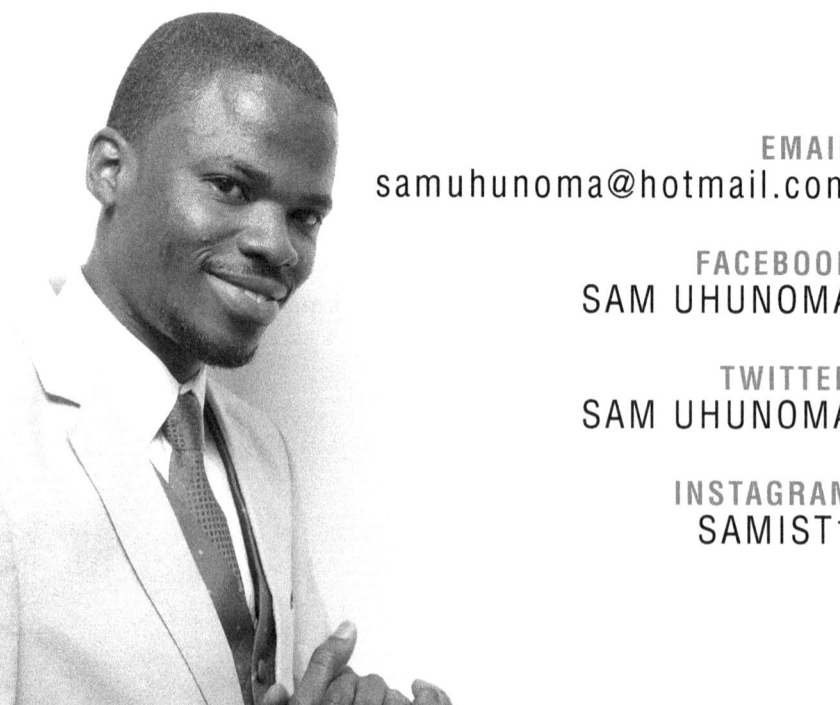

Note from the Publisher

Are you a first time author?

Not sure how to proceed to get your book published?
Want to keep all your rights and all your royalties?
Want it to look as good as a Top 10 publisher?
Need help with editing, layout, cover design?
Want it out there selling in 90 days or less?

Visit our website for some exciting new options!

www.chalfant-eckert-publishing.com

www.ingramcontent.com/pod-product-compliance
Lightning Source LLC
Chambersburg PA
CBHW070248100426
42743CB00011B/2186